HISTORY NOTES

Richard Wilcox

A STUDY GUIDE TO ACCOMPANY

THE
AMERICAN JOURNEY

VOLUME ONE

TEACHING AND LEARNING CLASSROOM EDITION
BRIEF THIRD EDITION

David Goldfield

Carl Abbott

Virginia DeJohn Anderson

Jo Ann E. Argersinger

Peter H. Argersinger

William L. Barney

Robert M. Weir

PEARSON

Prentice
Hall

Upper Saddle River, New Jersey 07458

© 2005 by PEARSON EDUCATION, INC.
Upper Saddle River, New Jersey 07458

10 9 8 7 6 5 4 3 2

ISBN 0-13-150107-0

Printed in the United States of America

CONTENTS

Chapter 1
Worlds Apart

Practice Test

1. Africans primarily came to early European settlements in America
    - A) voluntarily.
    - B) to find employment.
    - C) as slaves.
    - D) looking for trading partners.

2. What city was the center of Protestant reform in Europe?
    - A) London
    - B) Rome
    - C) Geneva
    - D) Paris

3. Meoamerica is the birthplace of
    - A) farming.
    - B) agriculture.
    - C) hunter-gatherer society.
    - D) aquatic exploration.

4. Archaeologists call the earliest Americans
    - A) Paleo-Indians.
    - B) Indios.
    - C) Native Americans.
    - D) Siberians.

5. Near the end of what period did some Indian peoples begin farming?
    - A) Archaic
    - B) Neo-Lithic
    - C) Jurassic
    - D) The Bronze Age

6. Which crop was NOT among those grown in America 5,000 years ago?
    - A) maize
    - B) pumpkins
    - C) squash
    - D) oranges

7. "Mound building" took the form of
    A) birds.
    B) serpents.
    C) humans.
    D) all of the above

8. Which group developed Mesoamerica's most advanced writing system?
    A) The Aztecs
    B) The Aleuts
    C) The Chinooks
    D) The Mayans

9. Which was the largest city in 1492?
    A) Laredo
    B) Mexico City
    C) Teotihuacan
    D) Rio Grande

10. Which group dominated Mexico from 900 to 1100 A.D.?
    A) The Aztecs
    B) The Mayans
    C) The Toltecs
    D) The Olmecs

11. The Aztec capital was
    A) Teotihuacan.
    B) Tenochtilan.
    C) Mesoamerica.
    D) Mexico City.

12. *Kivas* were special rooms used for
    A) Banquets.
    B) Schools.
    C) Religious ceremonies.
    D) Royal chambers.

13. Most Indians believed in
    A) Christianity.
    B) many gods.
    C) Hinduism.
    D) no religion.

14. This urban center dominated the Mississippi Valley.
    A) Cahokia
    B) New Orleans
    C) Adena-Hopewell
    D) St. Louis

15. The term *pueblo* means
    A) city.
    B) village.
    C) house.
    D) plain.

16. The histories of most early American people have been preserved in
    A) oral traditions.
    B) written documents.
    C) artwork.
    D) European records.

17. Cultures which trace their descent through the mother's family line are
    A) matriarchies.
    B) paternalistic.
    C) matrilineal.
    D) maternal.

18. Which of these was a great city of West Africa?
    A) Timbuktu
    B) Songhai
    C) Ghana
    D) Mali

19. Most West Africans were
    A) slaves.
    B) merchants.
    C) hunters.
    D) farmers.

20. Most African clans traced their descent through
    A) the father's lineage.
    B) the mother's lineage.
    C) matrilineal means.
    D) religious lines.

21. Which religion took root in West Africa in the eleventh century?
    A) Christianity
    B) Buddhism
    C) Islam
    D) Ancestor Worship

22. West Africans preserved their religious faith primarily through
    A) written sources.
    B) the construction of beautiful churches.
    C) oral tradition.
    D) song.

23. The majority of African slaves lost their freedom
    A) as punishment for crimes.
    B) because of debts.
    C) through trickery.
    D) by being captured in war.

24. What forces captured Morocco in 1415?
    A) Spanish
    B) English
    C) Portuguese
    D) French

25. The Renaissance originated in the city-states of
    A) Italy.
    B) Portugal.
    C) Greece.
    D) Spain.

When?

1. When did Islam spread in West Africa?
   A) 500 A.D.
   B) 1200 A.D.
   C) 1000 A.D.
   D) 1400 A.D.

2. What period marks the European Renaissance?
   A) 1400 – 1600 A.D.
   B) 800 – 1000 A.D.
   C) 1700 – 1800 A.D.
   D) 1100 – 1300 A.D.

3. When did Luther start the Protestant Reformation?
   A) 1417
   B) 1617
   C) 1517
   D) 1667

4. What year was the Treaty of Tordesillas?
   A) 1417
   B) 1500
   C) 1588
   D) 1494

5. When was the "Lost Colony" founded on Roanoke Island?
   A) 1587
   B) 1488
   C) 1642
   D) 1688

Where?

Matching

Match the explorer with the country that sponsored his expeditions.

Columbus	Portugal
Dias	France
De Leon	Spain
Drake	England
Raleigh	Holland
Cartier	Ireland
Cabot	
Da Gama	
Pizarro	
De Soto	

Map Labeling

Using this map from page 8, identify the areas in which the following primitive peoples lived:

The Mayans
The Susquehannocks
The Powhatans
The Pequots
The Aztecs

How and Why?

1. How did England's experience with the Irish influence their treatment of Indians?

2. How did England's difficulties with the Spanish affect their ability to establish a colony in the New World?

3. What were Columbus' goals when he began his expedition? Did he succeed in reaching them?

4. What factors contributed to the defeat of the Aztecs by Cortes?

5. Compare and contrast slavery in Africa and in America.

6. Discuss the cultural perceptions and misperceptions between Indians and European societies.

7. Analyze the differing interests each of the European powers had in the New World.

8. Which was a stronger force in New World colonization, economics or religion? Support your answer with specific examples.

9. Why were the events of the Renaissance important in setting the stage for New World exploration?

10. How did domestic European conflicts affect the actions of individual countries toward American exploration and settlement?

Chapter 2
Transplantation, 1600-1685

Practice Test

1. What was the one crop that attributed to the success of the new settlement of Jamestown?
    A) sugar
    B) cotton
    C) tobacco
    D) spices

2. What product was the economic base of New France?
    A) spice trade
    B) fur trade
    C) cotton
    D) sugar

3. Which was most important to the colony of New France?
    A) The St. Lawrence River
    B) Newfoundland
    C) Quebec
    D) Nova Scotia

4. Which product fueled the demand for furs in Europe in the early 1600s?
    A) mink stoles
    B) fur coats
    C) beaver fur hats
    D) otter fur pouches

5. What was the first permanent French settlement in Canada?
    A) St. Lawrence
    B) Quebec
    C) Toronto
    D) Newfoundland

6. King James I was petitioned to incorporate what two companies?
    A) Massachusetts Bay and Dutch East India
    B) West India and Massachusetts Bay
    C) Virginia and Plymouth
    D) Proprietary and Virginia

7. In early French settlements in America, there were
    A) more women than men.
    B) more men than women.
    C) roughly the same number of men as women.
    D) very many children.

8. Of the population of French settlers to North America how many returned to France?
    A) one out of ten
    B) two out of three
    C) three out of four
    D) five out of ten

9. What was the name of the first settlement in New England?
    A) Virginia Company
    B) Massachusetts Bay Colony
    C) Plymouth Company
    D) none of the above

10. Who did most of the work for French fur traders?
    A) African slaves
    B) indentured servants brought from France
    C) convicts
    D) Indians

11. French colonial governors were
    A) popularly elected.
    B) royal appointees.
    C) figure heads.
    D) independent of France's royalty.

12. French authorities
    A) encouraged continued westward expansion into North America.
    B) prohibited further westward expansion into North America.
    C) gave no military support to their American settlements.
    D) practiced benign neglect of their settlements.

13. Due to the presence of malaria in the James River region, how many of the original settlers survived in Jamestown in 1608?
    A) 75
    B) 38
    C) 52
    D) 27

14. What was the first settlement established by the Virginia Company?
    A) Roanoke
    B) Newfoundland
    C) Norfolk
    D) Jamestown

15. Who was the leader of the Jamestown settlement?
    A) Raleigh
    B) Smith
    C) James
    D) Champlain

16. What did the Lawes Divine Morall and the Martiall enforce?
    A) trading center Virginia
    B) the headright system
    C) the death penalty
    D) Joint Stock Company

17. Who was Pocahontas' husband?
    A) John Smith
    B) John Rolfe
    C) Powhatan
    D) Opechancanough

18. Who was Pocahontas' father?
    A) Powhatan
    B) Opechancanough
    C) Eneck-chak
    D) Pocahata

19. King James dissolved the Virginia Company in what year?
    A) 1622
    B) 1624
    C) 1626
    D) 1628

20. Catholics in Maryland were allowed to do ALL BUT the following?
    A) worship in public
    B) hold political office
    C) send their children to universities
    D) pass land on to heirs

21. Maryland was a
  A) joint stock company.
  B) headright system.
  C) proprietary colony.
  D) none of the above.

22. Which religious group believed the "Salvation is possible for all who heeded that 'Inner Light'"?
  A) Protestants
  B) Calvinists
  C) Quakers
  D) Lutherans

23. Those settlers who moved to the northern part of Carolina experienced problems producing what?
  A) tobacco
  B) rice
  C) tar
  D) pitch

24. In 1660s Charles II granted the development of ALL BUT what new colony?
  A) New York
  B) New Jersey
  C) Virginia
  D) Pennsylvania

25. Indentured servants received what for their labor?
  A) a steady wage
  B) free passage to Virginia
  C) a portion of the crops they harvested
  D) nothing

When?

Arrange the following colonies in the order they were founded from earliest to most recent:

  Maryland
  New Hampshire
  New York
  Rhode Island
  Virginia

Where?

Matching

Match the figure with his/her associated colony.

Penn	Rhode Island
Calvert	Massachusetts
Champlain	Virginia
Smith	Pennsylvania
Bradford	Quebec
Winthrop	Maryland
Williams	New Netherlands
Hutchinson	Carolina
Stuyvesant	
Cooper	

Map Skills

Using Map 2-1 in your text, answer the following questions.

1. What was the oldest settlement in New France?

2. Which settlement is farthest north in New France?

3. Most settlements in New France are along what river?

4. Where did most of the colonists in New France live?

5. The most northern portion of New France was called what?

How and Why?

1. Discuss the Puritans' beliefs and how they differed from Anglican practices.

2. What threat did Anne Hutchinson pose to the Massachusetts leadership?

3. How was agriculture in New England different than agriculture in the South?

4. Which crops contributed most heavily to the slave trade and why?

5. How did William Penn's religious background affect the way he treated his colonists?

6. Analyze the ways in which the various American colonies supported and restricted religious freedom.

7. Was it economic conditions or religious backgrounds that caused the North to rely so little on slavery, compared to the South?

8. What factors determined what kinds of relations the different groups of colonists had with the Indians?

9. Discuss how women contributed to the economy in early New England.

10. Analyze the role joint stock companies had in settling America.

Chapter 3
The Creation of New Worlds

Practice Test

1. What was the spark that started the Pueblo Revolt?
    A) religious persecution
    B) Spanish rule
    C) the drought
    D) raids by Apaches

2. Trade with European settlers
    A) was rejected by the Indians.
    B) unambiguously helped the Indians.
    C) helped to undermine the Indians' self-sufficiency.
    D) profited the Indians in no way.

3. The Stono Rebellion took place in which state?
    A) North Carolina
    B) South Carolina
    C) Georgia
    D) Florida

4. The Indians who traded with the Dutch in New Netherlands were devastated by what disease?
    A) Smallpox
    B) Typhoid
    C) Malaria
    D) Whooping Cough

5. Which tribe supported themselves by fishing?
    A) Iroquis
    B) Wampanoags
    C) Iroquois
    D) Micmacs

6. In the Spanish colonies, _____ is a grant to collect tribute from native peoples living on their land?
    A) repartimiento
    B) encomineda
    C) rescate
    D) abd

7. The Beaver Wars were fought between the Hurons and the
    A) Apaches.
    B) Cherokees.
    C) Micmacs.
    D) Iroquois.

8. By 1750, Native Americans had become a _____ of America north of the Rio Grande.
    A) minority of the inhabitants
    B) majority of the inhabitants
    C) group equal in size to European settlers
    D) group controlling the trade

9. The vast majority of African slaves ended up in all of the following areas EXCEPT
    A) Brazil.
    B) West Indies.
    C) Mainland Colonies
    D) New Spain

10. Which tribe was NOT part of the Iroquois League?
    A) Mohawks
    B) Hurons
    C) Senecas
    D) Oneidas

11. The French and the Dutch came to America mainly to
    A) trade.
    B) convert the Indians.
    C) found settlements.
    D) find religious freedom.

12. Why were the Hurons at a disadvantage in their battles with the Iroquois League?
    A) They were primarily pacifists.
    B) They were not well armed.
    C) They had no horses.
    D) They were not well organized.

13. Which group experienced the most violent conflicts with Indians?
    A) The French
    B) The Dutch
    C) The Quakers
    D) The English

14. Property rights among the Indians were held
   A) collectively.
   B) by the chief only.
   C) privately by individuals.
   D) by oral agreement.

15. William Penn acquired land from the Indians
   A) by force.
   B) through gambling.
   C) by paying for it.
   D) None of the above.

16. Who led the Pueblo Revolt?
   A) Pope
   B) Metacom
   C) Berkeley
   D) Logan

17. Spain's religious missionaries to America represented which religion?
   A) Catholicism
   B) Protestantism
   C) Quakerism
   D) Lutheranism

18. What was offered to the Pueblo by the Spanish as a reward for converting?
   A) tobacco
   B) farming implements
   C) protection against Apache raids
   D) land for future generations

19. People of mixed Indian and Spanish descent were called
   A) mestizos.
   B) mulattos.
   C) marzipans.
   D) makos.

20. Where were the participants of the Stono Rebellion headed?
   A) Georgia
   B) Massachusetts
   C) Florida
   D) Virginia

21. Who founded the "praying towns"?
    A) Roger Williams
    B) John Winthrop
    C) John Eliot
    D) William Penn

22. King Philip's War took place in
    A) Virginia.
    B) Carolina.
    C) Pennsylvania.
    D) New England.

23. Bacon's Rebellion took place in
    A) Virginia.
    B) Carolina.
    C) Pennsylvania.
    D) New England.

24. The Pueblo Revolt took place in
    A) New Mexico.
    B) Texas.
    C) Arizona.
    D) Colorado.

25. The English called which Indian leader King Philip?
    A) Massasoit
    B) Metacom
    C) Squanto
    D) Maroset

When?

1. The first Africans arrived in Virginia in
    A) 1419.
    B) 1519.
    C) 1619.
    D) 1719.

2. Georgia was established in
    A) 1632.
    B) 1682.
    C) 1732.
    D) 1782.

3. The Pequot War in New England took place in
   A) 1587.
   B) 1637.
   C) 1687.
   D) 1737.

4. The Stono Rebellion in South Carolina took place in
   A) 1639.
   B) 1689.
   C) 1739.
   D) 1789.

5. The Pueblo Revolt in New Mexico occurred in
   A) 1640.
   B) 1660.
   C) 1680.
   D) 1700.

Where?

Matching

Match the event with its proper date.

Maryland law defined slavery life-long inheratale status	1640
Tuscarora War in Carolina	1661
Second phase of the Beaver Wars	1711-1713
Yamasee War in Carolina	1741
Slave conspiracy discovered in New York City	1680
First phase of Beaver Wars	1715-1716

Map Skills

Use Maps 3-1A, B, and C to answer the following questions.

1. In which state are the Sangre De Cristo Mountains located?

2. Clergy from which religious order and from what country had missions located along the Chattahoochee River in Florida?

3. Clergy from which religious order and from what country had missions located along banks of the Great Lakes?

4. What current state was home to the Timucuas Indian tribe?

5. Along what river is Quebec located?

How and Why?

1. Describe how and why most slaves were brought to America.

2. How were the lives of slaves and indentured servants similar? Different?

3. Discuss the ways the Spanish exploited Native American labor.

4. How were many non-Africans "enslaved," in a sense, throughout America?

5. Explain the ways the Indians used trade relations to exert considerable influence over Europeans.

6. Analyze the evolution of the black family unit in America.

7. Was indentured servitude beneficial to those who entered into it?

8. In what ways did the colonists fear their slave labor force? Describe specific instances where their fears came true.

9. In what ways did geography and economics affect each colonial region's choice of labor supply?

10. Analyze the different attempts at conversion made by Protestants and Catholics in the New World. Which group was more successful and why?

Chapter 4
Convergence and Conflict, 1660s-1763

Practice Test

1. George Washington's family plantation was located in
    A) Monticello.
    B) Mount Vernon.
    C) Richmond.
    D) Jamestown.

2. Martha Washington's last name prior to marrying George was
    A) Todd.
    B) Buchanan.
    C) Custis.
    D) Jefferson.

3. In the 1700s, the most advanced economic power in Europe was
    A) Spain.
    B) France.
    C) England.
    D) Holland.

4. England's economic system between 1651 and 1733 could best be described as
    A) feudal.
    B) mercantilist.
    C) socialist.
    D) physiocratic.

5. The Navigation Act of 1651 required that
    A) all trade carried out in the English empire must be conducted in English ships.
    B) all maps be taxed at a high rate.
    C) all explorers register their voyages with Parliament.
    D) none of the above.

6. Between 1650 and 1770, the colonial economy grew
    A) more slowly than England's.
    B) at about the same rate as England's
    C) faster than England's.
    D) solely because of tobacco exports.

7. Which product was the most important colonial export?
   A) cotton
   B) rice
   C) tobacco
   D) sugar

8. Which crop was the most important agricultural export from mainland America?
   A) cotton
   B) rice
   C) tobacco
   D) sugar

9. Other than rice, what was South Carolina's most important crop?
   A) cotton
   B) tobacco
   C) indigo
   D) corn

10. All of the following EXCEPT _____ competed vigorously in transatlantic trade.
    A) England
    B) Spain
    C) Holland
    D) France

11. Which colonial region dominated transatlantic shipping?
    A) The Carolinas
    B) The West Indies
    C) New England
    D) New York

12. Merchants brought sugar by-products back to New England to be distilled into
    A) schnapps.
    B) vodka.
    C) gin.
    D) rum.

13. The colonies under mercantilist legislation
    A) suffered.
    B) prospered.
    C) were unaffected.
    D) prospered, then suffered.

14. The colonists were net _____ of manufactured goods.
    A) exporters
    B) importers
    C) users
    D) suppliers

15. English merchants _____ credit to colonists.
    A) were reluctant to extend
    B) generously extended
    C) were barred by law from extending
    D) none of the above

16. By 1770, the largest British provincial town was
    A) New York.
    B) Boston.
    C) Charleston.
    D) Philadelphia.

17. The University of Pennsylvania in Philadelphia was originally chartered as
    A) Pennsylvania State University.
    B) Benjamin Franklin University.
    C) The College of Philadelphia.
    D) Pennsylvania College.

18. The male residents of colonial cities were primarily
    A) unemployed.
    B) farmers.
    C) sailors.
    D) artisans.

19. Which city was described as "most flourishing" and "with much the air of some of our best country towns in England"?
    A) Boston
    B) Philadelphia
    C) New York
    D) none of the above

20. Once an apprentice completed his training, he became a
    A) senior apprentice.
    B) journeyman.
    C) master.
    D) unionist.

21. During the 18th century, the gap between the rich and poor in the colonies
    A) narrowed.
    B) widened.
    C) disappeared.
    D) remained constant.

22. The majority of colonists _____ the styles and culture of the British elite.
    A) believed American styles and culture were superior to
    B) believed American styles and culture were inferior to
    C) had little interest in copying
    D) were ignorant of

23. 18th century America imported _____ English manufactured goods than it did previously.
    A) fewer
    B) fewer (on a per capita basis)
    C) more (on a per capita basis)
    D) about the same number of (on a per capita basis)

24. The 18th century Governor's Palace of Virginia was located in
    A) Williamsburg.
    B) Jamestown.
    C) Richmond.
    D) Norfolk.

25. Colonists built grand houses not only to advertise their wealth, but also to
    A) show how they were different from their British counterparts.
    B) emulate the English gentry in their country.
    C) keep up with their fellow colonists.
    D) none of the above.

When?

Arrange the following wars in their proper order starting with the earliest.

King George's War.
King William's War.
The French and Indian War.
Queen Anne's War.
The Seven Years' War.

Where?

Matching
Match the war's English name with the name given to it in the Colonies

<u>English Name</u>   <u>Name in the Colonies</u>

War of the Spanish Succession   French and Indian War
War of Austrian Succession   King William's War
War of the League of Augsburg   Queen Anne's War
 Seven Year's War   King George's War

Map Labeling

Use Map 4-1 from the text to answer the following questions.

1. Where was rum produced?

2. What tradable goods did England produce?

3. What did Africa trade to pay for its imports?

4. What goods did New England export?

5. What exports came from the Lower South?

How and Why?

1. In what ways did Enlightenment thinking break down the importance of organized religion?

2. Discuss the impact the Great Awakening had on religious views in the North and in the South.

3. How did political representation differ in the colonies and in England?

4. Describe the relationship backcountry settlers had with the Indians.

5. Describe the importance of shipping to the New England economy.

6. Describe the role of taxation in the development of colonial notions of personal liberties.

7. Analyze the role British styles and culture played for colonial elites and commoners.

8. Analyze the effects of the mercantilist economic system. Who benefited and who was hurt and why?

9. Analyze why the colonists rejected the Albany Plan of Union.

10. Analyze the ultimate effects of the Treaty of Paris (1763) on the American colonies.

Chapter 5
Imperial Breakdown, 1763-1774

Practice Test

1. At the end of the French and Indian War, which country gained possession of East Florida?
>   A) Spain
>   B) France
>   C) England
>   D) Portugal

2. At the end of the French and Indian War, which country gained possession of Cuba?
>   A) Spain
>   B) France
>   C) England
>   D) Portugal

3. At the end of the French and Indian War, which country gained possession of Louisiana?
>   A) Spain
>   B) France
>   C) England
>   D) Portugal

4. Spanish officials appointed to ensure better colonial tax collection were called
>   A) viceroys.
>   B) attendants.
>   C) intendants.
>   D) none of the above.

5. Spain expelled which religious order from its colonial dominions?
>   A) Franciscans
>   B) Dominicans
>   C) Augustinians
>   D) Jesuits

6. At the end of the French and Indian War, which country had the most powerful military?
>   A) France
>   B) Spain
>   C) England
>   D) Portugal

7. The colonists _____ the Quartering Acts.
   A) supported
   B) did not support
   C) remained indifferent
   D) none of the above

8. The Cherokees agreed to settle land in which two states as an agreement in the Cherokee War?
   A) Maine and Massachusetts
   B) Florida and Georgia
   C) Carolina and Virginia
   D) Virginia and Maryland

9. The Proclamation of 1763 forbade white settlement
   A) in Canada.
   B) in Louisiana.
   C) west of the Appalachians.
   D) west of the Rockies.

10. The Quartering Acts required
    A) colonial assemblies be reduced in size by 75%.
    B) colonial assemblies to provide barracks for British troops.
    C) colonial assemblies to remit one fourth of tax revenues to England.
    D) none of the above.

11. One of the main goals of The Proclamation of 1763 was to
    A) maintain peace with the Indians.
    B) prevent missionaries from settling in new territories.
    C) curb unauthorized trade.
    D) ensure better tax collection.

12. After the French and Indian War, European alliances with the Indians
    A) became more important.
    B) all broke down.
    C) became less important.
    D) were strengthened.

13. The Cherokee War took place where?
    A) Florida
    B) New England
    C) The southern Appalachian highlands
    D) The Mississippi River

14. In 1760, the Cherokees captured
    A) Fort Loudoun.
    B) Fort Duquesne.
    C) New Orleans.
    D) Fort McHenry.

15. Neolin, who urged Indians to reject European goods and influence, was known as
    A) the Pennsylvania Prophet.
    B) the Ohio Prophet.
    C) the Delaware Prophet.
    D) the Maryland Prophet.

16. Pontiac, who led the Indians against the colonists and British troops was a(n) _____ chief.
    A) Ottawa
    B) Cherokee
    C) Delaware
    D) Oneida

17. The Paxton Boys massacred a group of which Indians?
    A) Delawares
    B) Oneidas
    C) Conestogas
    D) Cherokees

18. Who convinced the Paxton Boys to disperse as they threatened the Pennsylvania Assembly?
    A) Penn
    B) Franklin
    C) Hamilton
    D) Washington

19. The Two Penny Act involved Anglican ministers in which colony?
    A) Pennsylvania
    B) Maryland
    C) Virginia
    D) New York

20. In the cases brought by the Two Penny Act, which man defended the colonial government?
    A) Benjamin Franklin
    B) Thomas Jefferson
    C) George Washington
    D) Patrick Henry

21. Which act prohibited the colonies from printing their own legal tender paper money?
   A) The Sugar Act
   B) The Stamp Act
   C) The American Revenue Act
   D) The Currency Act of 1764

22. The American Revenue Act was commonly known as
   A) The Stamp Act.
   B) The Navigation Act.
   C) The Sugar Act.
   D) The Corn act.

23. Who was the British Prime Minister that passed the American Revenue Act in 1764?
   A) Chamberlain
   B) Grenville
   C) Churchill
   D) Cromwell

24. What one issue placed the biggest strain on the relationship between the colonies and the empire?
   A) freedom
   B) taxation
   C) loyalty
   D) none of the above

25. Which act was the first to impose an internal tax on the colonies?
   A) The Sugar Act
   B) The Stamp Act
   C) The Navigation Act
   D) The Tea Act

When?

Place the following events in the proper order beginning with the earliest.

George III becomes king
Boston Tea Party
Stamp Act passed
Townshend duties imposed
Paxton Boys murder Conestogas

Where?

Matching

Match the event/figures with the place with which it is primarily associated.

Pontiac's Rebellion	Harrisburg
Paxton Boys	Virginia
Parson's Cause	Philadelphia
Stamp Act Congress	New York City
First Continental Congress	Ohio Valley
Regulators	Boston
Dartmouth	North Carolina

Map Skills

Use Map 5-1 from the text to answer the following questions.

1. What mountain range did the Proclamation Line of 1763 follow?

2. What river formed the eastern boundary of Spanish territory in 1763?

3. What was the purpose of the Proclamation Line of 1763?

4. What Indian tribes resided in West Florida in 1763?

5. What Indian tribes resided in the Province of Quebec in 1763?

How and Why?

1. How did the British and the colonists view the French and Indian War differently?

2. What was the Boston Tea Party meant to protest?

3. What events led to the need for the First Continental Congress?

4. How were the taxes enacted in the Stamp Act different than taxes previously imposed on the colonists?

5. Who was hurt by the Quebec Act?

6. How did the British and the American ways of viewing representative government differ? How did these differences lead to problems between England and America?

7. How did most colonists hope to handle America's difficulties with England? Why did they hold these views and why did they think such tactics would be successful?

8. What did the British hope to achieve with the Quebec Act?

9. Describe relations between the Indians and the various European and colonial powers in the period just prior to the American Revolution. How did these relations differ from those of earlier periods?

10. How did the different colonies react to the Sugar Act and the Stamp Act? Why was the Stamp Act more offensive to the colonists than the Sugar Act?

Chapter 6
The War for Independence, 1774-1783

Practice Test

1. Who headed the Massachusetts Committee of Safety in 1774?
    A) Samuel Adams
    B) John Adams
    C) John Hancock
    D) Paul Revere

2. The Conciliatory Proposition pledged not to tax the colonists if
    A) they swore allegiance to the king.
    B) they purchased all of their finished goods from England.
    C) they would quarter British troops in America.
    D) they voluntarily contributed to the defense of the empire.

3. Gage and his troops were given orders to arrest John Hancock and whom on April 18, 1775?
    A) John Adams
    B) Samuel Adams
    C) Paul Revere
    D) Ethan Allen

4. In 1774-1775 as the threat of _____ mounted, the Loyalists and Whigs began to part company.
    A) taxation
    B) loyalty to the crown
    C) war
    D) none of the above

5. The first American casualties of the Revolutionary War were killed in
    A) Lexington.
    B) Concord.
    C) Boston.
    D) Philadelphia.

6. Who dubbed the first shot fired in Lexington as the "shot heard round the world?"
    A) Emerson
    B) Irving
    C) Whitman
    D) Longfellow

7. The Second Continental Congress was held in
   A) Boston.
   B) New York.
   C) Philadelphia
   D) Annapolis.

8. At the start of the Revolutionary War, who commanded militia forces from Massachusetts?
   A) Ethan Allen
   B) Benedict Arnold
   C) John Adams
   D) Paul Revere

9. In 1774-1775 Americans dragged cannons some 300 miles from Fort Ticonderoga to what city?
   A) Boston
   B) Norfolk
   C) Washington
   D) Charleston

10. What document asserted American patriots would "die freemen, rather than live as slaves"?
    A) the Olive Branch Petition
    B) the Declaration of Independence
    C) the Constitution
    D) the Declaration of the Causes and Necessity of Taking Up Arms

11. Who was named commander of the Continental Army?
    A) George Washington
    B) Benedict Arnold
    C) Paul Revere
    D) John Adams

12. Of what battle did a British officer remark that another such victory "would have ruined us"?
    A) Battle of Lexington
    B) Battle of Concord
    C) Battle of Fort Ticonderoga
    D) Battle of Bunker Hill

13. In March 1776, the British evacuated their troops from Boston and moved to
    A) Providence.
    B) Halifax.
    C) New Haven.
    D) Portland.

14. King George III's actions to deny the colonists protection and parliament's decision to bar all exports from the American colons caused
    A) the colonists to cease fighting.
    B) the Whigs to think more seriously about declaring their independence from Britain.
    C) the colonists to import more goods.
    D) the colonists to seriously consider an Anglo-American reconciliation.

15. The pro-independence pamphlet *Common Sense* was written by
    A) Franklin.
    B) Jefferson.
    C) Paine.
    D) Madison.

16. Who composed the first draft of the Declaration of Independence?
    A) John Adams
    B) Thomas Jefferson
    C) Thomas Paine
    D) George Washington

17. Congress voted on the Declaration of Independence on
    A) July 2, 1776.
    B) July 3, 1776.
    C) July 4, 1776.
    D) July 5, 1776.

18. In the phrase "life, liberty, and the pursuit of happiness" the third element was originally
    A) happiness.
    B) equality.
    C) property.
    D) democracy.

19. Most Whigs subscribed to the political ideology known as
    A) republicanism.
    B) statism.
    C) libertarianism.
    D) liberalism.

20. _____ is derived from the political ideas of classical antiquity.
    A) Despotism
    B) Republicanism
    C) Democracy
    D) Federalism

21. German mercenaries were called what by the Americans?
    A) Prussians
    B) Badens
    C) Bavarians
    D) Hessians

22. The nickname for British soldiers was
    A) Limeys.
    B) Brits.
    C) Redcoats.
    D) Brown Bessies.

23. Benedict Arnold offered to surrender what to the British?
    A) West Point
    B) Annapolis
    C) Valley Forge
    D) Providence

24. Generally speaking, all of the following Indian groups supported the British during the War EXCEPT for
    A) the Mohawks.
    B) the Cherokees.
    C) the Choctaws.
    D) the Oneidas.

25. During the late colonial period, the headquarters of the British Army in America was in
    A) Boston.
    B) New York.
    C) Philadelphia.
    D) Norfolk.

When?

Place the following events in their proper order beginning with the earliest.

Declaration of Independence is ratified
Battle of Bunker Hill
Thomas Paine's *Common Sense* is published
Battle of Lexington
Battle of Trenton

Where?

Matching

Match the battle with the colony in which it took place.

Charleston   New York
Moore's Creek Bridge   New Jersey
Great Bridge   Pennsylvania
Bunker Hill   Massachusetts
Lexington   Virginia
Concord   North Carolina
Trenton   South Carolina
White Plains
Brandywine Creek
Saratoga

Map Skills

Use Map 6-2 in your text to answer the following questions.

1. From which direction did Montgomery attack Quebec?

2. From which direction did Arnold attack Quebec?

3. Which colony saw the earliest fighting?

4. To which colony did present day Maine belong?

5. Who won the battle of Great Bridge?

How and Why?

1. Why was the American victory at Saratoga particularly important?

2. Why did the Americans' fighting style give them an advantage over British forces?

3. How did the writings of John Locke influence the Declaration of Independence?

4. Why did Benedict Arnold offer to help the British?

5. How did the war lead to inflation in the colonies?

6. Why was Washington selected by Adams to command the Continental Army? What made him the ideal person for the job?

7. What role did marginalized groups (e.g., blacks, Indians, and women etc.) play in the war for both sides? Were any of these groups left better off after the war ended?

8. Analyze Benjamin Franklin's role in securing American independence.

9. Compare and contrast 3 areas of difference between the life of an American soldier and a British soldier.

10. Why was the much larger and better-supported British military defeated?

Chapter 7
The First Republic, 1776-1789

Practice Test

1. All of the following are true about the rebels of Shays's Rebellion EXCEPT:
    A) Many of them were vulnerable to the point of losing their farms
    B) They felt overburdened by the taxes saddled upon them by the state legislature
    C) A low supply of currency denied them the proper means for economic recovery
    D) Frustration did not cause them to resent the policies and views of the elite

2. The Articles of Confederation were ratified in
    A) 1780.
    B) 1781.
    C) 1783.
    D) 1785.

3. When a Spanish officer, Francisco de Miranda, witnessed a war victory celebration in North Carolina, he was astonished by
    A) the natural mixing of social classes at the affair.
    B) the participants' lack of enthusiasm.
    C) the absence of drinking as a form of celebration.
    D) the fact that Americans still drank a toast to King George.

4. How many slaves gained freedom as a result of the war?
    A) about 15,000
    B) about 35,000
    C) about 50,000
    D) about 75,000

5. New York ended slavery in
    A) 1772.
    B) 1782.
    C) 1785.
    D) 1799.

6. As a result of the Revolution,
    A) the number of free blacks increased dramatically.
    B) the number of slaves in the South dropped.
    C) slaves grew less bold in their efforts to gain freedom.
    D) slaves stopped running away in the 1800's.

7. Between 1777 and 1784,

    A) many states allowed women the momentary right to vote.

    B) most northern states accelerated their use of slavery.

    C) slaveowners resorted to the use of Indian slaves.

    D) most northern states ended slavery.

8. At the end of the war, a British officer observed, "they have made all their world their enemies by their attachment to us." Who does "they" refer to in this statement?

    A) Anglo-Americans who were Tories

    B) Leaders of the American Revolution

    C) Canadians who were loyal to England

    D) Native Americans who lost England as an ally

9. Most state constitutions, put into effect by the end of 1777, included all of the following EXCEPT:

    A) the curbing of the powers of the governor in the states.

    B) the establishment of annual elections as a norm.

    C) a form of a bill of rights to set limits on government interference with private citizens.

    D) a commitment to custom rather than written constitutions.

10. Which state constitution served as the model for those to follow?

    A) Pennsylvania

    B) Georgia

    C) New York

    D) Connecticut

11. The most democratic constitution of the revolutionary period was passed in

    A) Pennsylvania.

    B) New York.

    C) South Carolina.

    D) Massachusetts.

12. Framers of the Pennsylvania Constitution of 1776 established

    A) a constitutional monarchy.

    B) a one-house legislature without an executive officer.

    C) the right to vote for all people 21 or older.

    D) a system which narrowed voting rights for the duration of the war.

13. A *unicameral* legislature is

    A) the dominant power in all constitutional monarchies.

    B) a one-house system of government.

    C) the foundation of federal republicanism.

    D) the key ingredient of bicameral governments.

14. Under the Articles of Confederation, the American states were
    A) bound by strict statutes of economic and trade policies.
    B) had little power compared to the national government.
    C) subject to the rule of the national judiciary.
    D) created as a loose association of autonomous states.

15. Under the Articles of Confederation, the national government could NOT
    A) raise an army.
    B) conduct foreign affairs.
    C) declare war.
    D) negotiate with Native Americans.

16. The central forces behind the Articles of Confederation
    A) were mainly reluctant supporters of the Revolution.
    B) feared the encroachment of a powerful, centralized government.
    C) were Tories who sabotaged the American war effort.
    D) asserted that the President should have final say on all matters.

17. By the end of the war, Continental money was
    A) actively invested in the London stock exchange.
    B) used to effectively pay off the nation's war debts.
    C) virtually worthless.
    D) more valuable than the British pound.

18. The Bank of North America, the nation's first bank, was located in which city?
    A) New York
    B) Boston
    C) Philadelphia
    D) none of the above

19. The leader of the economic nationalists was
    A) Thomas Jefferson.
    B) Patrick Henry.
    C) Robert Morris.
    D) William Paterson.

20. After the Revolution, British merchants
    A) canceled all debts owed to them by American merchants.
    B) continued to close its markets to American goods.
    C) refused to sell goods to consumers in America.
    D) eagerly accepted Continental money as a means of payment.

21. Within a year of the surrender of Great Britain, the American economy
    A) experienced the nation's first depression.
    B) thrived due to subsidies from France.
    C) experienced a surplus of exports over imports.
    D) bolstered the strength of the small family farm.

22. The depression of the 1780s included all of the following EXCEPT:
    A) a stagnant economy.
    B) a burdensome debt.
    C) booming trade with North Americans.
    D) a growing population.

23. In order to combat the mounting debt incurred by the war, debtors wanted states to issue paper money to settle their debts because
    A) they didn't have hard currency.
    B) paper money was easier to procure.
    C) paper money would have an inflationary effect, raising wages and the prices of farms commodities, and reducing the value of debts contracted in hard currency.
    D) None of the above.

24. The _____ forced the Iroquois Confederacy of New York to cede half of its territory to the United States.
    A) Treaty of Fort Stanwix
    B) Treaty of Fort McIntosh
    C) Land Ordinance of 1785
    D) Southwest Ordinance of 1790

25. The Northwest Ordinance applied to the national domain north of what river?
    A) Mississippi
    B) Potomac
    C) Ohio
    D) St. Lawrence

When?

1. Which is the only event that happened during the Revolutionary War?
    A) Shays's Rebellion
    B) the Virginia Plan is proposed
    C) the Annapolis Convention convenes
    D) the Articles of Confederation are proposed

2. All of the following happened after the British surrender in the Revolutionary War EXCEPT:

A) the onset of an economic depression in America.

B) Shays's Rebellion.

C) large number of farmers in Massachusetts lost their land.

D) states began writing their own constitutions.

3. What is the correct order of events?

A) Bank of North America created, Shays's Rebellion, Constitution ratified

B) Constitution ratified, Shays's Rebellion, Bank of North America created

C) Shays's Rebellion, Bank of North America created, Constitution ratified

D) Shays's Rebellion, Constitution ratified, Bank of North America created

4. Which event happened last?

A) Constitutional Convention ends

B) Bill of Rights enacted

C) Shays's Rebellion

D) Jay-Gardoqui Treaty defeated

Where?

Matching

Match the figure with his home state.

Alexander Hamilton	New York
Roger Sherman	Massachusetts
Robert Morris	Pennsylvania
Theophilus Parsons	Virginia
George Mason	South Carolina
Edmund Randolph	Connecticut
John Hancock	
James Madison	
Patrick Henry	
Edward Rutledge	
James Monroe	

How and Why?

1. What characteristics define American republicanism?

2. What was the major difference of opinion between Federalists and Antifederalists?

3. What sort of men made up the membership of the Constitutional Convention?

4. Why did Southerners vehemently oppose the Jay-Gardoqui Treaty?

5. What motivations caused the creation of the Bank of North America?

6. Compare and contrast the major differences between the United States Constitution and the State Constitution of Pennsylvania created in 1776.

7. Explain why the Great Compromise was adapted over the New Jersey Plan.

8. What major problems did the young republic face after its victory over Great Britain? How did these problems motivate members of the elite to call for a federal constitution?

9. Support the following statement that, to you, best expresses the creation of the Constitution.

"The creation of the Constitution represented...

1) ...a remarkable example of constructive compromise."

2) ...great vision for the nation's future by the men who created it."

3) ...a successful attempt by the commercial elite to place themselves in power."

4) ...accommodation of both conservative and liberal visions of republicanism."

10. The Virginia Plan replaced the Confederation Congress. List and explain two factors that differed from the Confederation Congress.

Chapter 8
A New Republic and the Rise of Parties, 1789-1800

Practice Test

1. At the time of George Washington's first inauguration, all of the following were true EXCEPT:
    A) two states had not yet ratified the Constitution.
    B) political parties were already bitterly opposed to each other.
    C) the government faced a huge debt.
    D) conditions in the West were unstable.

2. The national census of 1790 revealed that the number of white and black Americans was
    A) 2,500,000.
    B) 4,000,000.
    C) 10,000,000.
    D) 25,000,000.

3. There was little use of indentured servants or slaves in New England because
    A) Quakers had the strongest influence of governments in the region.
    B) most of the region's people were involved in manufacturing.
    C) the government of Massachusetts never allowed either practice.
    D) it was an impractical place to cultivate cash crops.

4. New England was the most uniform region in America for all of the following reasons EXCEPT:
    A) it contained the highest percentage of people who had been Loyalists.
    B) Puritan values continued to be a dominant force in cultural identity.
    C) Most New Englanders' ethnic heritage was English.
    D) Very few blacks or Indians lived in the region.

5. What was different about the population of New England compared to other regions?
    A) Women outnumbered men in parts of the region.
    B) It had the largest percentage of free blacks in America.
    C) Catholics and Quakers made up a great deal of the population.
    D) New Englanders exhibited the widest range of social diversity.

6. The most ethnically and religiously diverse region in early America was
    A) New England.
    B) the Deep South.
    C) the Carolinas.
    D) the Mid-Atlantic region.

7. _____ was the first state, in 1789, to allocate funds for girls' elementary education.

    A) Connecticut
    B) Rhode Island
    C) Massachusetts
    D) Vermont

8. A major source of profit in the Mid-Atlantic was
    A) commercial farming of wheat.
    B) transportation of British imports.
    C) plantation cultivation of tobacco.
    D) rice farming.

9. Mid-Atlantic culture was characterized by all of the following EXCEPT:
    A) serving as the "breadbasket" of American farming.
    B) a rich diversity of ethnicity and religion throughout the region.
    C) a wider job market than existed in New England.
    D) a clear consensus for republicanism with a strong central government.

10. What factor made the South the most populous region in the early United States?
    A) the most beneficial job market in the nation
    B) the comfortable climate for doing outdoor labor
    C) the appeal of a wide range of European-American cultures
    D) the presence of a large number of African-American slaves

11. Freeing slaves was made easier by all the following EXCEPT
    A) revolutionary values of liberty effected moral sensibilities
    B) rewards for enlisting services in war
    C) laws were passed to make it easier to free slaves
    D) due to the concentration of slaves in the south, many had fought in the war and died.

12. Which geographic region best describes the American West in 1790?
    A) from the Appalachian Mountains to the southern Canadian border
    B) from the Blue Ridge Mountains to the Atlantic Ocean
    C) from the Appalachian Mountains to the Mississippi River
    D) from the Mississippi River to the Pacific Ocean.

13. The West offered settlers the opportunity of all the following EXCEPT:
    A) own their own farms
    B) gain economic independence
    C) alleviate the competition of slave labor
    D) high survival rate for settlers children.

14. *Squatters*
   A) owned the first plantations in the West.
   B) occupied land even though they held no title on it.
   C) always enjoyed good relations with Native Americans.
   D) tended to come from the richest sectors of southern society.

15. Who was seen as the leader in the House in the fight to satisfy both Federalists and the Antifederalists? (educated men)?
   A) Hamilton
   B) Madison
   C) Franklin
   D) Washington

16. Federalists fought for all the following EXCEPT
   A) individual rights
   B) state's rights
   C) restrictions on personal liberties
   D) imposition of a uniform national culture

17. John Adams proposed that George Washington be addressed as
   A) "Mr. President."
   B) "Republican."
   C) "His Highness."
   D) "Sir George."

18. The Bill of Rights became part of the Constitution on
   A) December 1, 1791.
   B) November 12, 1792.
   C) December 15, 1790.
   D) December 15, 1791.

19. The first government's base support was strengthened by
   A) stopping Fries's Rebellion.
   B) repealing the Sedition Act.
   C) passing the Bill of Rights.
   D) calming Southerners with Jay's Treaty.

20. Congress increased the power of the President when it allowed the executive to
   A) nominate and dismiss officials in the presidential cabinet.
   B) establish foreign trade policies without Congressional approval.
   C) appoint cabinet officers without Congressional approval.
   D) author and interpret the Bill of Rights.

21. The Judiciary Act
    A) was a heavy-handed move for power by the Federalists.
    B) showed that Southerners would never compromise on judicial powers.
    C) represented an artful compromise that balanced legal powers.
    D) was designed primarily to raise revenues.

22. Within the Bill of Rights, how many amendments spoke to the interest of the state?
    A) 1
    B) 2
    C) 3
    D) 5

23. Madison wanted to place especially high duty taxes on imports from
    A) France.
    B) England.
    C) Germany.
    D) Canada.

24. The first Secretary of Treasury was
    A) Thomas Jefferson.
    B) James Madison.
    C) Alexander Hamilton.
    D) John Jay.

25. Hamilton proposed a series of reports to solve the financial woes after the war, which included all of the following EXCEPT:
    A) a bold plan to address the Revolutionary War debt.
    B) an excise tax.
    C) government should not promote industry.
    D) the chartering of a national bank.

When?

1. Which event did not happen during Washington's presidency?
    A) passage of the Bill of Rights
    B) the Battle of Fallen Timbers
    C) passage of the Sedition Act
    D) ratification of Jay's Treaty

2. Which is the correct order of events?
    A) Hamilton submits financial plan, Adams elected, Whiskey Rebellion
    B) Whiskey Rebellion, Adams elected, Hamilton submits financial plan
    C) Hamilton submits financial plan, Whiskey Rebellion, Adams elected
    D) Whiskey Rebellion, Hamilton submits financial plan, Adams elected

3. Which headline would have appeared in 1800?
   A) "Washington Warns of Divisiveness in Farewell Address"
   B) "American Troops Enter Pennsylvania Seeking Whiskey Rebels"
   C) "Southern Leaders Outraged by Jay's Treaty"
   D) "Thomas Jefferson Elected as New President in Tight Election"

4. Washington was inaugurated in
   A) 1785.
   B) 1789.
   C) 1795.
   D) 1796.

5. Diplomatic relations with France were improved in
   A) 1794.
   B) 1796.
   C) 1798.
   D) 1800.

Where?

Matching

Match the party with what they supported

FEDERALISTS   Supported Hamilton's economic program
REPUBLICANS   Generally supported French Revolution
                         Strongest support from south and west
                         Supported Jay's Treaty
                         Opposed Alien and Sedition Acts

Map Skills

Use Map 8-1 from your text to answer the following questions.

1. Name three Indian tribes that lived in Spanish Louisiana.

2. Where was Fort Miami located?

3. Where did St. Clair's defeat take place?

4. What section of America did the Indians cede almost entirely before 1784?

5. What Indian tribes lived in British North America during this time period?

How and Why?

1. What facts reveal that New England was the most uniform cultural area of early America?

2. What factors made the mid-Atlantic region the nation's first breadbasket?

3. What civil liberties are guaranteed in the Bill of Rights? How did the Bill of Rights come to be included as the first amendments to the Constitution?

4. What were the major problems that confronted the Washington administration?

5. Why was there a split in the Federalist Party in the period, 1796-1800?

6. How did life in America's four regions reveal both the differences and shared values among the citizens of the early republic?

7. What were the key causes and events that illustrate that the 1790s was a decade of growing partisanship in American politics?

8. Hamilton had a vision that manufacturing, like a national currency, would be a great national unifier. Explain and provide support for this vision.

9. What were the different visions of America expressed by Federalists and the Republicans?

10. What developments of the 1790's resulted in the rise of the Republican Party? What mistakes did the Federalists make?

Chapter 9
The Triumph and Collapse of Jeffersonian Republicanism, 1800-1824

Practice Test

1. All of the following belonged to the Republican Party EXCEPT:
    A) Thomas Jefferson.
    B) John Adams.
    C) James Monroe.
    D) James Madison.

2. Thomas Jefferson's vision for the future of America included all of the following EXCEPT:
    A) a citizenry that placed public good over private gain.
    B) a nation without slavery in which blacks and whites lived in natural harmony.
    C) the view that the white farmer represented the ideal republican citizen.
    D) a republic that shunned the rigid social hierarchy of a corrupt Europe.

3. Successes of Jefferson's first term included all of the following EXCEPT:
    A) a reduction in the size of the federal government.
    B) getting rid of the Alien and Sedition Acts.
    C) purchasing the Louisiana Territory.
    D) a successful embargo on foreign trade.

4. The style of Thomas Jefferson's inauguration revealed that
    A) republicanism would replace the aristocratic formalities of the Federalists.
    B) although he was devoted to democracy, he enjoyed the frills of aristocratic ceremony.
    C) he no longer contemplated the ideals of the American Revolution.
    D) the concerns of rural America were not a major priority of his administration.

5. Albert Gallatin, Jefferson's Secretary of the Treasury, did all of the following EXCEPT:
    A) reduced the National debt.
    B) eliminated internal taxes.
    C) repealed the Whiskey Tax.
    D) boosted military budget.

6. Thomas Jefferson showed a more democratic style by doing all of the following EXCEPT:
    A) not wearing a wig in the style of the upper class.
    B) supporting the right to vote for women and free blacks.
    C) walking to his inauguration rather than riding in a carriage.
    D) disregarding aristocratic seating at state dinners.

7. In his handling of the Barbary pirates and the purchase of Louisiana, Jefferson
    A) showed that he still was a strict constitutional constructionist.
    B) revealed that expansion of the American economy was not a high priority.
    C) established that he would assertively use his presidential powers.
    D) relied upon his belief in peaceful coercion.

8. Aaron Burr's presidential bid was thwarted by the work of
    A) Jefferson.
    B) Hamilton.
    C) Madison.
    D) Wilkinson.

9. Prior to the Louisiana Purchase, Thomas Jefferson
    A) attempted to make an anti-British alliance with Napoleon.
    B) withdrew all American troops from the Mississippi Valley.
    C) tried to slow the migration of American farmers into the Louisiana Territory.
    D) sent Lewis and Clark on an expedition through upper Louisiana.

10. All of the following statements about the Louisiana Purchase are true EXCEPT:
    A) it was opposed by many Federalist legislators.
    B) it revealed President Jefferson's aggressive style in supporting national interests.
    C) it doubled the size of the United States.
    D) it contained a great deal of America's least productive farmland.

11. The United States bought the Louisiana Territory for an average cost per acre of
    A) 3 1/2 cents.
    B) 25 cents.
    C) $3.50.
    D) $25.00.

12. In order to eliminate the threat of French dominance in America, Jefferson did all of the following BUT:
    A) strengthened American forces in the Mississippi Valley
    B) received congressional approval for Lewis & Clark's expedition through Louisiana
    C) cut off talks with Britain
    D) opened exploratory talks with the British

13. At the start of the War of 1812, the Americans
    A) fought nobly.
    B) outwitted their opponents easily.
    C) pathetically executed Madison's vision.
    D) none of the above.

14. Napoleon entered into a secret treaty with which country in 1800 to reacquire the Louisiana Territory?
    A) Britain
    B) US
    C) France
    D) Spain

15. "The Star Spangled Banner" was written during what war?
    A) The American Revolution
    B) The War of 1812
    C) The Chesapeake Affair
    D) none of the above

16. Who was the hero of the Battle of New Orleans?
    A) Monroe
    B) Madison
    C) Jackson
    D) Packenham

17. Who provoked the Battle of Tippecanoe?
    A) Tecumseh
    B) Harrison
    C) the British
    D) young braves

18. The Era of Good Feelings is typically considered the time period of
    A) 1811-1815.
    B) 1814-1816.
    C) 1817-1823.
    D) 1818-1825.

19. Supporters of the War of 1812 were mainly from what regions?
    A) North and East
    B) West and East
    C) South and West
    D) East and South

20. During the war period of 1793-1807 between England and France, American merchants

       A) sided with England.

       B) ceased trading with European nations.

       C) enjoyed a huge increase in profits for exports.

       D) struggled through the effects of economic depression.

21. Which statement about the Embargo Act of 1807 is NOT true?

       A) It resulted in a vibrant economic boom in America.

       B) It represented President Jefferson's belief in "peaceable coercion."

       C) It prohibited merchants from trading with Europe.

       D) It failed to cause England and France to change their trade policies.

22. Which of the following was NOT a factor that pushed America into war with England?

       A) Napoleon's duplicity in terms of shipping decrees

       B) the reimposition of nonintercourse against the British

       C) mounting frustrations in the South and West

       D) mounting frustrations in the North

23. The _____ emerged from the War of 1812 more powerful than ever.

       A) Federalists

       B) Republicans

       C) British

       D) Loyalists

24. The War Hawks from the South and the West were led by whom?

       A) Calhoun

       B) Madison

       C) Clay

       D) Cone

25. President Madison was embarrassed when

       A) the Madison-Erskine agreement was disavowed by England.

       B) he was defeated in his first run for the presidency.

       C) the Americans lost the Battle of New Orleans.

       D) Napoleon refused to talk to him about trade issues.

When?

1. What is the correct order of presidential terms?

       A) Jefferson, Madison, Monroe

       B) Monroe, Jefferson, Madison

       C) Jefferson, Monroe, Madison

       D) Monroe, Madison, Jefferson

2. Which event happened last?
  A) President Jefferson purchased Louisiana.
  B) James Madison elected president.
  C) Great Britain surrendered to end the War of 1812.
  D) Andrew Jackson and his troops defeated the Creek Indians.

3. Which event happened after 1820?
  A) Americans won the Battle of New Orleans.
  B) President Monroe was elected to his first term.
  C) A "corrupt bargain" defeated Andrew Jackson.
  D) The Treaty of Ghent was signed.

4. Which headline would have appeared in 1820?
  A) "War Hawks Cry for Conflict Over Disputed Territories"
  B) "Jefferson Announces Embargo on Trade to Europe"
  C) "Clay Works to Calm Passions Regarding Slavery"
  D) "Westerners, Southerners Protest 'Corrupt Bargain'"

5. Which event happened last?
  A) America declared war on England.
  B) Rush-Bagot Agreement was signed.
  C) Jefferson announced trade embargo.
  D) Treaty of Ghent was signed.

Where?

Matching

Match the 1824 presidential candidate with his home state.

John Calhoun   Georgia
William Crawford   Kentucky
John Quincy Adams   Massachusetts
Henry Clay   South Carolina
Andrew Jackson   Tennessee

Map Skills

Use Map 9-1 from your text to answer the following questions.

1. In which city did Lewis and Clark's expedition begin?

2. What was the most western point of Lewis and Clark's journey?

3. What river did Lewis and Clark follow from the beginning of their journey until they reached their winter quarters of 1804-1805?

4. How did Lewis and Clark differ from each other in their return routes?

5. Which country controlled the land west of the Rio Grande in 1803?

How and Why?

1. How did President Jefferson immediately show a difference in style compared to his Federalist predecessors?

2. What factors caused the Federalists to quickly fall out of favor with American voters?

3. What were the key military turning points in the Americans' victory in the War of 1812?

4. How did the Missouri Compromise attempt to soothe the growing disputes over slavery?

5. What incidents revealed the American government's growing aggressiveness in its relations with Native Americans?

6. How successful was Thomas Jefferson in living up to his republican ideals during his two terms as president?

7. Analyze the vital role that foreign relations played in the presidential administrations of 1800-1824.

8. What were the main causes and consequences of the War of 1812?

9. What evidence reveals that sectional differences regarding the economy and allocation of political power were growing in the period 1809-1824?

10. Who was the most effective and influential president in the period 1800-1824? Cite evidence that supports your choice.

Chapter 10
The Jacksonian Era, 1824-1845

Practice Test

1. Jacksonian Democrats believed all of the following ideas EXCEPT:
   A) their party should oppose aristocratic privilege.
   B) morality should be promoted through their party.
   C) farmers and workers should be protected from the economic elite.
   D) the Bank of the United States represented the interests of the elite.

2. _____ was defined as the majority rule of white males.
   A) Democracy
   B) Republicanism
   C) Political democracy
   D) None of the above.

3. After the Salary Act of 1816,
   A) Andrew Jackson was elected president in the next election.
   B) American workers received higher wages.
   C) many Congressmen were voted out of office in the next election.
   D) John Calhoun emerged as a major spokesman for the working class.

4. By the end of the 1820's, the right to vote
   A) was restricted to wealthy white males.
   B) was available to less Americans than were eligible in 1800.
   C) had moved significantly toward universal manhood suffrage for whites.
   D) was extended to include blacks and females in the North.

5. In the 1820's, supporters of universal manhood suffrage believed that
   A) the president should make decisions without considering the will of the people.
   B) personal liberties should be guarded by political participation of all white men.
   C) Andrew Jackson did not support their political and economic interests.
   D) southern states should secede from the union.

6. Which group was an active participant in the Second Great Awakening?
   A) Traditional Calvinists
   B) Roman Catholics
   C) Congregational Presbyterians
   D) Baptists

7. In terms of voting, _____ were/was the norm by the 1820s.
   A) written ballots
   B) stand-up voting
   C) oral voting
   D) election by state legislators

8. Many evangelical preachers of the Second Great Awakening
   A) were wealthy Federalists.
   B) saw no connection between religion and the common person.
   C) emphasized a solemn approach to religion.
   D) directly challenged slavery.

9. Which phrase best summarizes the impact of the Second Great Awakening?
   A) "Salvation for all white males"
   B) "God cast no favors upon the common man"
   C) "Salvation open to all"
   D) "Catholicism is the new way of America"

10. The first presidential candidate of the Democratic Party was
    A) James Monroe.
    B) Andrew Jackson.
    C) Henry Clay.
    D) John C. Calhoun.

11. All of the following statements are true about Andrew Jackson's background EXCEPT:
    A) he was of Scots-Irish ancestry.
    B) he was born and raised in the southern backcountry.
    C) achieving a college education led him to eventual success.
    D) military heroism elevated his image in the popular mind.

12. An important legacy of the election of 1824 was
    A) Jackson's election as the "people's president."
    B) large-scale spending can win an election.
    C) public sympathy for Jackson who lost because of a "corrupt bargain."
    D) the expression of slavery as a major issue in American elections.

13. Jacksonians portrayed John Quincy Adams as a man who
    A) fulfilled the noblest goals of the Revolution.
    B) represented the interests of the yeoman farmer.
    C) would never do anything about slavery.
    D) was arrogant and did not understand the common man.

14. The Albany Regency, a tightly disciplined political machine, was run by
    A) John Quincy Adams.
    B) Martin Van Buren.
    C) John Tyler.
    D) Nelson Biddle.

15. In the election of 1828, Adams ran well only
    A) in New England.
    B) with ordinary Americans
    C) in Massachusetts and New York City.
    D) with farmers of the South and West.

16. Jackson established the Democrats as all of the following EXCEPT:
    A) the friend(s) of the common man
    B) proponents of market-minded entrepreneurs
    C) enemy of special privilege
    D) defenders of the Union.

17. Jackson's political opponents viewed his inauguration as "vulgar" because
    A) he decided to have the inauguration held in his native Carolina.
    B) common people took part in the festivities at the White House.
    C) in his speech, Jackson threatened to even the wealth between the East and the South.
    D) the new president used off-color humor in his inaugural address.

18. The *spoils system* features a strategy in which
    A) government jobs are given to supporters of the victorious party.
    B) large land speculators have the strongest influence in government.
    C) the military is aggressively used as a factor in foreign relations.
    D) the Bank of the United States is the central facet of the economy.

19. Which policy was supported by Andrew Jackson?
    A) wide use of protective tariffs
    B) support of a strong national bank
    C) internal improvements that benefited the general public
    D) large government subsidies to bolster manufacturing

20. The Cherokee Indians
    A) had a written language and a constitution.
    B) were seen by whites as the most savage tribe in the South.
    C) always refused to assimilate with white culture.
    D) never experienced significant grievances with white political authorities.

21. An honest appraisal of Jackson's Indian policies reveals that
    A) he was a benevolent "white father" of the Indians.
    B) he was considerate of Indian interests.
    C) he ignored political legislation in favor of military action.
    D) he believed in forced removal after getting legislation passed.

22. The term *Trail of Tears* refers to
    A) the horrifying conditions experienced by Cherokees during their removal.
    B) the plight of the yeoman farmer in the face of industrial power.
    C) the slaughter of the Sauk and Fox Indians in northern Illinois.
    D) the system of separating families through the slave trade in the Deep South.

23. What was Black Hawk's War?
    A) a battle between the Sauk and Fox tribes
    B) a battle between the Indians and the U.S. Army
    C) a frantic attempt by the Indians to reach the bank of the Mississippi River
    D) a battle between the Seminoles and the U.S. Army

24. In the case *Worcester vs. Georgia*, the Supreme Court ruled that
    A) the Bank of the United States was unconstitutional.
    B) slavery was an issue left to the discretion of individual states.
    C) the state of Georgia had violated the Constitution in their treatment of Indians.
    D) Jackson's Indian policies were constitutional and within his rights of executive action.

25. Which statement would most likely been said by a supporter of *nullification*?
    A) "Our union, it must be preserved above all else and at all costs."
    B) "The promotion of the nation's industrial base is the foundation of our republic."
    C) "The states shall not adhere to federal law that is deemed to be unconstitutional."
    D) "As the nation grows in size, a strong central government is a vital necessity."

When?

1. What is the correct order of events?
    A) Pakenham letter, Texas annexed, Polk elected
    B) Polk elected, Pakenham letter, Texas annexed
    C) Pakenham letter, Polk elected, Texas annexed
    D) Texas annexed, Pakenham letter, Polk elected

2. The only event that happened in the 1830's was
    A) the removal of Indian tribes from the South.
    B) the annexation of Texas.
    C) the death of President Harrison.
    D) the Webster-Ashburton Treaty.

3. Which event happened first?
   A) Jackson opposed renewal of the charter for the Bank of the United States.
   B) The Panic of 1837 illustrated the depth of the country's depression.
   C) Federal employees were given a ten-hour workday.
   D) The first Whig president was elected.

4. Which headline would have appeared in 1844?
   A) "Whigs expel president from their party"
   B) "Supreme Court Challenges Jackson's Indian Policy"
   C) "Panic in Financial Markets Paralyzes National Economy"
   D) "Polk Downs Clay in Close Election"

5. Which is the only event that happened in the 1840's?
   A) Polk ran for president on expansionist ideas.
   B) Nat Turner lead slave rebellion in Virginia.
   C) The American Anti-Slavery Society was founded.
   D) William Lloyd Garrison began publishing *The Liberator*.

Where?

Matching

Match the states with the candidate winning their electoral votes in the 1828 election.

Pennsylvania	Andrew Jackson
Tennessee	John Quincy Adams
New Hampshire	
Georgia	
Kentucky	

Map Skills

Use Map 10-1 from your text to answer the following questions.

1. In what year were the Seminoles removed from Florida?

2. What tribe was removed in 1838?

3. The Seminoles left Florida for which state originally?

4. Which tribe's eventual removal journey was longest?

5. Which tribes lived farthest north before being removed?

How and Why?

1. What was the base of the strong political coalition developed by Andrew Jackson?

2. Why was Andrew Jackson popular with voters in the South and West?

3. What was the appeal of the Anti-Masons as a third political party?

4. What ideas personified the beliefs of the Whig Party in 1840?

5. What was the philosophy of those who supported nullification and the gag rule?

6. What is your assessment of the presidency of Andrew Jackson? Do you view his presidency as more of a success or more of a failure?

7. How was it becoming apparent that sectionalism and the issue of slavery were becoming vital and heated political topics in American society?

8. What was the Eaton Affair and how did it violate the political rules that women were expected to follow?

9. How did the annexation of Texas emerge as an important political issue? Why were the Democrats more in favor of expansion than the Whigs?

10. Why was Jackson so adamant in dissolving the Bank of the United States? In your opinion, was this a wise decision? Why or why not?

Chapter 11
Slavery and the Old South, 1800-1860

Practice Test

1. All of the following factors made the Lower South ideal for growing cotton EXCEPT:
   A) long growing season.
   B) white southerners' willingness to work the land.
   C) navigable rivers.
   D) untapped fertility.

2. Before 1800, slavery was associated with all of the following cash crops EXCEPT
   A) rice.
   B) sugar.
   C) tobacco.
   D) long-staple cotton.

3. By the late 1700's, a long-range disadvantage of cultivating tobacco was
   A) great numbers of Americans and Europeans no longer smoked tobacco.
   B) the American government stopped the exportation of tobacco.
   C) the quality of American tobacco had become harsh and dry-tasting.
   D) the soil of the Upper South had become depleted of vital nutrients.

4. The use of widescale slavery in the Lower South was based on the economic production of
   A) rice.
   B) short-staple cotton.
   C) tobacco.
   D) long-staple cotton.

5. All of the following states were in the heart of the *cotton kingdom* EXCEPT
   A) Texas.
   B) Mississippi.
   C) South Carolina.
   D) Virginia.

6. What percentage of the white southern population belonged to the plantation-owning class?
   A) <5%
   B) >12%
   C) <20%
   D) >32%

7. The most-valued slaves in the slave market of 1815-1850 were male field hands and
    A) older males who had years of experience working in cotton fields of the Lower South.
    B) males who possessed the skills of an artisan such as carpentry and engraving.
    C) older females who acted as matriarchs within slave communities.
    D) females of child-bearing age as a way of increasing the slave population.

8. In 1808, the United States Congress
    A) ended the African slave trade.
    B) passed national slave codes.
    C) required that slaves be Christians.
    D) classified slaves as citizens.

9. A particularly cruel aspect of the internal slave trade was that it
    A) required minimum sale prices.
    B) resulted in the passing of slave codes.
    C) separated slaves from their families.
    D) only sold slaves from the Upper South.

10. From 1820-1860 slaves decreased by what percentage of the urban population?
    A) 50% to 30%
    B) 37% to 15%
    C) 22% to 10%
    D) 17% to 12%

11. All of the following statements about urban slavery are true EXCEPT
    A) it increased dramatically in the years leading to the Civil War.
    B) urban slaves often lived apart from their owners.
    C) it allowed slaves much more freedom of social interaction.
    D) urban slaves could sometimes hire out their labor for wages.

12. Southern planters believed that the system of slavery would be weakened by
    A) government subsidies.
    B) an increase in the internal slave trade.
    C) the use of short-staple cotton.
    D) free labor.

13. In 1860, what was the population of the South? What percentage of the nation's manufacturing output did it account for?
    A) 1/2; 60%
    B) 1/3; 10%
    C) 1/3; 25%
    D) 1/3; 15%

14. *Marl* was used in the attempt to
  A) build an industrial base in the South.
  B) replenish the soil in the Upper South.
  C) resume an economy based on long-staple cotton.
  D) pay off debts owed on farm mortgages.

15. By mid-century, the Upper South
  A) accounted for only a small percentage of southern industry.
  B) no longer expressed the philosophy of state's rights.
  C) had diversified its economy and relied less on slavery.
  D) failed to attract immigrants from the North.

16. Which statement about slavery in the Upper South from 1815-1850 is NOT true?
  A) Many small farmers became indifferent or opposed to the institution of slavery.
  B) The region served as a major exporter of slaves to the Lower South.
  C) Slavery did significantly increase in any of the region's states except Arkansas.
  D) Wheat failed as a cash crop because it required intense labor done by more slaves.

17. All of the following statements about *slave codes* are true EXCEPT
  A) they were only enacted in the cotton kingdom of the Lower South.
  B) they authorized whippings as a common form of punishment.
  C) most codes did not recognize marriages between slaves as legal.
  D) many slave states declared it was illegal to teach slaves to read or write.

18. The general health of slaves included all of the following factors EXCEPT
  A) a diet that provided ample calories but poor nutrition.
  B) a life expectancy that was roughly the same as their white contemporaries.
  C) chronic suffering of intestinal disorders.
  D) an extraordinarily high infant mortality rate.

19. The housing of slaves revealed that
  A) owners tried to keep slaves pleased about their living conditions.
  B) slaves' homes were larger than middle-class dwellings of the North.
  C) owners, in this area, tried to create an atmosphere of individuality.
  D) housing was meager and provided little more than basic shelter.

20. Slave owners commonly used all of the following incentives to motivate hard work EXCEPT
  A) the insincere promise of eventual freedom.
  B) the transfer from field slave to house slave.
  C) the promises of extra rations or time off.
  D) the spread of fear through whippings.

21. _____ was the one state that recognized slave marriages.
    A) Georgia
    B) South Carolina
    C) Texas
    D) Louisiana

22. Roughly one-third of slave marriages were
    A) recognized as legal by southern law.
    B) ended by informal consent of the married couple.
    C) based on a family unit that included a permanent father.
    D) broken up by sales or forced removals.

23. Slaves followed West African customs in all of the following ways except
    A) keeping alive a rich folklore and oral tradition.
    B) rejecting extended kinship ties.
    C) prohibiting marriages between cousins.
    D) fusing the natural and spiritual worlds in religious beliefs.

24. In West African culture, which art form was linked with ancestry and considered sacred?
    A) pottery making
    B) dancing
    C) painting
    D) written literature

25. It is estimated that what percentage of slaves converted to Christianity?
    A) 10%
    B) 20%
    C) 30%
    D) 40%

When?

1. Which event happened first?
    A) Eli Whitney invented the cotton gin.
    B) Congress banned the African slave trade.
    C) Virginia's legislature considered gradual emancipation.
    D) Texas was admitted as a slave state.

2. In which year did Gabriel Prosser lead a rebellion in Richmond, Virginia?
    A) 1788
    B) 1800
    C) 1831
    D) 1857

3. Which event happened last?

A) Thomas Dew published his full-scale defense of slavery.

B) Nat Turner lead a rebellion in Virginia.

C) Florida and Texas were admitted as slave states.

D) Congress prohibited the African slave trade.

4. When did Virginia legislature debate and then reject gradual emancipation?

A) 1816-1819

B) 1822-1824

C) 1831-1832

D) 1837-1845

5 Which headline would have appeared in the 1850s?

A) "Virginia Legislature Heatedly Debates Gradual End to Slavery"

B) "Turner's Rebellion Kills 60, Stuns South"

C) "Planters Meet to Discuss Possible Split from Union"

D) "Jackson Crushes South Over Nullification"

Where?

Matching

Match the region with the year in which it held the highest percentage of total slaves in the U.S.

Lower South	1800
Upper South, Middle States	1830
Upper South, Border States	1860

Map Skills

Use Map 11-2 from the text to answer the following questions.

1. In which states was hemp a major crop in 1860?

2. What were the major crops of Alabama in 1860?

3. Which states produced tobacco?

4. Where was sugar cane grown in the U.S. in 1860?

5. Where was cotton the primary crop in 1860?

How and Why?

1. Name 3 reasons why it was generally more efficient to own a plantation versus a small farm for harvesting cotton.

2. Describe the three-tiered hierarchy of race that existed in the South.

3. Discuss the ways slaves maintained a sense of dignity and self-respect. Were their attempts successful? Why or why not?

4. Describe the responsibilities and lifestyle of women who were married to plantation owners.

5. Which slaves were regarded as most valuable on the slave market?

6. What conditions personified the typical lifestyle of a plantation slave?

7. In what ways did slaves nurture the survival of West African culture as a part of their African-American culture?

8. What profound changes in slavery occurred in the period 1815-1860? What were the causes and consequences of this significant shift?

9. What changes occurred in the southern economy in the first half of the nineteenth century? What factors accounted for these changes?

10. How did southern whites attempt to defend slavery and reconcile it with their Christian beliefs? Why did they feel compelled to express these defenses?

Chapter 12
The Market Revolution and Social Reform, 1815-1850

Practice Test

1. By 1850, manufacturing accounted for _____ of total commodity output.
   A) 1/4
   B) 1/3
   C) 1/2
   D) none of the above

2. An effect of the practical use of steamboats was
   A) a drop in trade between the West and the South.
   B) rendering canals obsolete.
   C) a revolution in transportation on western rivers.
   D) the onset of an economic depression in the East.

3. The first demonstration of the practical commercial use of the steamboat was achieved by
   A) Samuel Slater.
   B) Walt Whitman.
   C) Samuel Morse.
   D) Robert Fulton.

4. The idea for the Erie Canal
   A) originated with New York legislature who wished to reach the agricultural West.
   B) was created by Southerners, looking for new cotton markets in Central America.
   C) was rejected by Congressmen from the commercial Northeast.
   D) led to few job opportunities for immigrant workers.

5. The _____railroad line opened in England in 1825.
   A) Baltimore and Ohio
   B) Sussex and Oxford
   C) Stockton and Darlington
   D) Union and Pacific

6. The success of the Erie Canal was
   A) an isolated example of canal-building in the 1800s.
   B) achieved despite the increase in transportation costs along the canal.
   C) a key factor in developing close economic ties between the East and West.
   D) celebrated by New Yorkers in ceremonies that honored the Irish workers who built it.

7. During the 1840s,
    A) canals emerged as the most efficient form of commercial transportation.
    B) railroads became the most dynamic booster of interregional trade.
    C) rail connections helped establish close economic ties between the Northeast and South.
    D) canals moved trade much faster and for less capital investment than railroads.

8. During the 1840's, American railroads
    A) experienced a tripling in miles of tracks.
    B) developed steadily but slowly.
    C) became commercially centered in the South.
    D) did not equal the miles of railways developed in Europe.

9. Half of all capital for early railroads
    A) came from state governments.
    B) was invested by the federal government.
    C) came from European investors.
    D) was generated by southern investors.

10. The court system's support of corporate rights to *eminent domain* meant that
    A) investors were protected from creditors if a corporation went bankrupt.
    B) canals could only be constructed with capital provided by the federal government.
    C) interstate commerce could not be supervised by the federal government.
    D) corporations could purchase "rights of way" land whenever they needed it.

11. In *Gibbons v. Ogden*, the Supreme Court ruled that
    A) states could not restrict trade within their jurisdictions.
    B) rail companies could not purchase farmland without the consent of farmers.
    C) monopolies were better for the public good than open competition.
    D) the national government had no say in supervising interstate commerce.

12. _____ contributed to the expansion of industrialism after the War of 1812.
    A) Loans to start new businesses
    B) Cheap labor
    C) High immigration population
    D) The establishment of mercantile centers

13. Which was not among America's largest cities in 1820?
    A) New York
    B) Philadelphia
    C) Baltimore
    D) Pittsburgh

14. By the 1850s, the West accounted for what percentage of the nation's manufacturing output?
    A) 10%
    B) 20%
    C) 25%
    D) 50%

15. Who spread the word that salvation was available to those who willed it?
    A) Evans
    B) Gibbons
    C) Finney
    D) Astor

16. The Sabbatarian movement focused on
    A) making it illegal to produce and sell alcohol.
    B) abolishing slavery through gradualist legislation.
    C) making reading of the Bible mandatory in schools.
    D) stopping commerce and leisure activities on Sunday.

17. The Democratic Congress of 1829 upheld the postal law of 1810 based on
    A) the concept of separation of church and state.
    B) the First Amendment of the Constitution.
    C) the philosophy of transcendentalism.
    D) a commitment to state's rights.

18. Which statement best describes Americans' consumption of alcohol in the era 1800-1830?
    A) The consumption of alcohol was confined to the working class.
    B) Americans consumed alcohol at a much greater rate than today.
    C) Americans of the 1600s drank more than those of the eerily's.
    D) The consumption of alcohol was not a major part of the national culture.

19. Temperance made inroads with the working class during
    A) the War of 1812.
    B) the presidency of Thomas Jefferson.
    C) the Era of Good Feelings.
    D) the depression of 1839-1843.

20. Leaders of populist religious sects believed that the leaders of benevolent reform
    A) were the nation's moral backbone.
    B) represented an elite that was trying to control the morals of the nation.
    C) were the best spokesmen of America's local communities.
    D) should be elected to Congress.

21. The Mormons
    A) believed that evangelical churches had fragmented the male-centered rural culture.
    B) were mainly commercial farmers with origins in the Upper South.
    C) believed that benevolent reform should be guided by both males and females.
    D) were convinced that tithes represented the greed and corruption of evangelical leaders.

22. *The Book of Mormon* was authored by
    A) Lyman Beecher.
    B) Robert Owen.
    C) Joseph Smith.
    D) Theodore Dwight Weld.

23. Horace Mann believed that public education
    A) should be provided only for the professional class.
    B) would be the great equalizer in American society.
    C) should promote the virtues of the Roman Catholic Church.
    D) would never work in New England.

24. Horace Mann's ideas for public education included all of the following EXCEPT:
    A) the use of common textbooks.
    B) requirements of compulsory attendance.
    C) professionally trained teachers.
    D) national control of the state schools.

25. Horace Mann's vision of public education received great support from
    A) the hierarchy of the Roman Catholic Church.
    B) the business constituency of the Whig Party.
    C) the yeoman farmers of the West.
    D) planters in the emerging Lower South.

When?

Directions: Fill in the letter of the decade with its correct event for numbers 1 through 5.

A= 1820s   B= 1830s   C= 1840s

1. _____ The Erie Canal is completed.

2. _____ Starvation begins mass migration of Irish to the United States.

3. _____ In *Gibbons v. Ogden*, the Supreme Court acts against state monopolies.

4. _____ American Temperance Society begins crusade

5. _____ The first national trade union is created.

Directions: Answer the following multiple-choice questions.

6. Which event happened first?
    A) The American Colonization Society was formed.
    B) The Liberty Party ran a candidate for president.
    C) Congress passed a gag rule.
    D) David Walker published his *Appeal*.

7. Which headline would have appeared in 1848?
    A) "Leading Abolitionist Killed by Mob in Illinois"
    B) "'New' Women Declare Themselves Free at Convention"
    C) Antislavery Forces Angered by Passing of 'Gag Rule'"
    D) "Joseph Smith, Mormons Begin 'Trek to Freedom'"

Where?

Matching

Match the reform movement type with its best example

Moral	Shakers
Institutional	Seneca Falls
Utopian	American Antislavery
Abolitionist	Massachusetts Board of Education
Women's Rights	American Temperance Society

Map Skills

Use Map 12-1 from your text to answer the following questions.

1. In what state was the Genesee Turnpike located?

2. What city marked the western end of the National Road?

3. In what state was the Lancaster Turnpike located?

4. What three rivers meet in Pittsburgh?

5. What canals were located in New York?

How and Why?

1. What characteristics describe the Rhode Island system and the Waltham system?

2. What were the most important improvements in transportation during the first half of the nineteenth century?

3. How were the economic interests of the West linked with those of the Northeast?

4. According to nativists, what problems plagued America?

5. In what ways can it be said that new divisions between "North" and "South" were developing in America during the period 1800-1850?

6. Why did economic growth widen the gap between the rich and the poor?

7. Discuss the factory system of production. Why was it an advantageous system?

8. How can the rapid surge of American industrialism in the period 1815-1850 be explained?

9. Address the following statement: "The rapid growth of industrialism spurred both progress and conflict."

10. What was the goal of the Temperance movement? Was this movement a success? If so, how?

11. What was the Slave Power and how did it reflect growing sectionalism?

12. Choose from three of the following abolitionists and analyze their contributions to the movement:

William Lloyd Garrison, Frederick Douglass, David Walker, Lydia Maria Child, Theodore Dwight Weld, the Grimke sisters

13. What evidence reveals the emergence of women as a major force in movements for social reform in American history?

14. In what ways to did institutional reformers change American practices regarding prisons, asylums, and workhouses?

15. In what ways did abolitionists frame the moral argument regarding slavery in the period 1815-1850?

Chapter 13
The Way West

Practice Test

1. Which statement would most likely have been said by a believer in *manifest destiny*?
    A) "It is our God-given right to spread our democracy and culture across the continent."
    B) "It is only through Christian kindness that we can achieve peace with the Indians."
    C) "The ways of the factory represent America's greatest hope for a better future."
    D) "God can never rest easy with our nation until we challenge and defeat slavery."

2. The forces that pushed many Americans westward included all of the following EXCEPT
    A) scarcity of land in the East, especially New England.
    B) economic inequality was high in the East.
    C) commercial farmers of the East and South were struggling financially.
    D) the land of the West was fertile, abundant, and relatively inexpensive.

3. During the years of the Jeffersonian Republicans, the government's land policies
    A) focused mainly on the commercial farmers of the mid-Atlantic region.
    B) attempted to aid Americans who wished to become freeholders.
    C) made it more difficult for small farmers to purchase land in the West.
    D) guaranteed that a migrant farmer in the West would become wealthy.

4. A consistent pattern of movement into the Old Northwest was
    A) the tendency of Northerners and Southerners to settle, respectively, in northern and southern sections of the Old Northwest.
    B) the loss of northern and southern cultural practices and identities as migrants settled without considering regional concerns.
    C) less antagonism regarding the issue of slavery because virtually all migrants to the Old Northwest were members of the Whig Party.
    D) to bypass attempts to become a small freeholder, and buy large amounts of cheap land in the attempt to establish a commercial farm.

5. Local associations known as *claims clubs*
    A) enforced extralegal property rights for squatters.
    B) promoted an increase in profits for speculators.
    C) worked to stop slavery from spreading to the West.
    D) showed the national government's commitment to promoting slavery.

6. Which product became the Old Northwest's major cash crop for the northern market?
    A) corn
    B) hogs
    C) wheat
    D) soybeans

7. Westerners promoted industrialization in the East
    A) by providing food for the growing workforce of the East.
    B) by demonstrating methods of industrial success in western iron mills.
    C) by sending many young people to work in eastern factories.
    D) by investing large amounts of capital in eastern manufacturing.

8. Which state in the Old Northwest was the last one to gain statehood?
    A) Ohio
    B) Wisconsin
    C) Illinois
    D) Indiana

9. What pattern in the location of slavery occurred in the period 1790-1860?
    A) an increase in the overall percentage of slavery located in the South Atlantic region
    B) a decrease in the use of slaves in both the South Atlantic and Old Southwest regions
    C) a rejection of the use of slavery in the Old Southwest while it increased elsewhere
    D) a large movement of slavery from the South Atlantic to the Old Southwest

10. *Short-staple cotton* became a major profit-maker for all of the following reasons EXCEPT
    A) Eli Whitney's cotton gin made it easier to remove its abundant amount of sticky seeds.
    B) it could be grown easily in various growing conditions.
    C) the majority of settlers in the Old Southwest owned large plantations that grew it.
    D) England was a major market for the product.

11. What was the yeoman's chief force of labor?
    A) slaves
    B) freemen
    C) stock herders
    D) his immediate family

12. By the 1840s, over half the value of American exports was derived from
    A) corn.
    B) cotton.
    C) rice.
    D) wheat.

13. In the 1850s, all of the following states EXCEPT _____ were core states of the Old Southwest.
    A) Kentucky
    B) Oklahoma
    C) Tennessee
    D) Mississippi

14. Whites had originally been reluctant to settle on the western Plains because
    A) they had no desire to see the spread of freehold farming.
    B) they felt guilty about displacing eastern Indians into that region.
    C) they believed the region had little potential for agriculture.
    D) land on the western Plains was extraordinarily expensive.

15. All of the following hunting and raiding tribes lived on the open plains EXCEPT the
    A) western Sioux.
    B) Crows.
    C) Arapahos.
    D) Hidatsas.

16. At the end of Black Hawk's War, which state was opened to white settlement and forced tribes to turnover their land?
    A) Kansas
    B) Iowa
    C) Oklahoma
    D) Oregon

17. Before 1850, who was the dominant power on the north and central Great Plains?
    A) Whites who had migrated from the South
    B) the Cherokees who had been removed from their homeland
    C) the United States cavalry
    D) the warrior-hunters of the Sioux tribe

18. What differences in the fighting of war existed between whites and the Plains Indians?
    A) The Plains Indians rejected the white man's use of horses in battle.
    B) Whites often engaged in war while the Plains Indians were pacifists.
    C) The Plains Indians fought to show honor rather than killing many enemies.
    D) Whites fought for moral reasons and never for the control of land.

19. What was *counting coup*?
    A) a way of recording land claims in the West
    B) an Indian practice of showing skill in battle
    C) a currency used by both whites and Indians in the West
    D) the Indian practice of scalping whites

20. What were the two products traded by branches of the Sioux tribe at the yearly trade fair?
    A) buffalo robes and corn
    B) corn and rifles
    C) horses and beaver pelts
    D) beaver pelts and buffalo robes

21. Conditions for white fur-traders included all of the following EXCEPT
    A) brutal living conditions in the wilderness.
    B) more economic and cultural ties than other whites had with Indians.
    C) close ties with the economic elite of the Northeast who dominated the fur trade.
    D) exploration of many trails and paths on the frontier.

22. Even under ideal conditions, the journey on the Oregon Trail took about
    A) two weeks.
    B) two months.
    C) six months.
    D) one year.

23. A treaty signed in 1818 created joint control of the Oregon Territory by the United States
    A) and France.
    B) and the Nez Perce Indians.
    C) and the Sioux Indians.
    D) and England.

24. The smallest group of people that made up 1 of the 4 groupings in Mexico were
    A) Mestizos.
    B) the Spanish.
    C) Criollos.
    D) Indians.

25. The Fort Laramie Treaty included all of the following EXCEPT:
    A) The Sioux received treaty rights to lands south of the Platte.
    B) The U.S. government drew boundaries to contain Plains Indians.
    C) An annual compensation of $50,000 per year for 50 years.
    D) Returned land to the Kiowas and Crows.

When?

Directions: Fill in the letter of the year with its correct description.

A= 1806   B= 1821   C= 1836   D= 1844   E= 1848

1. _____ First large parties of migrants set out on the Oregon Trail.

2. _____ Lewis and Clark return from their journeys into the West.

3. _____ Stephen F. Austin establishes the first American colony in Texas.

4. _____ The Treaty of Guadalupe Hidalgo ends the Mexican War.

5. _____ Texas wins independence from Mexico

Where?

Matching

Match the state with its slave status when it entered the Union.

Indiana
Missouri
Iowa
Florida
California   Slave
Arkansas   Free
Texas
Mississippi
Michigan
Alabama

Map Skills

Use Maps 13-1A, B, and C to arrange these places in the correct order moving from east to west.

Sutter's Fort
Bent's Old Fort
Fort Hall
Fort Laramie
Fort Kearney

How and Why?

1. What did Americans mean by Manifest Destiny?

2. Define the following terms: *mestizo*, *criollo*, *Californio*, and *Tejano*.

3. Why did President Jefferson tell Lewis and Clark to "cultivate good relations with the Sioux"? How did Lewis and Clark describe this large tribe on the Great Plains?

4. In what way did Manifest Destiny combine with the pride that some Americans felt in their Anglo cultural roots?

5. Why did the location of American slavery shift in the period 1790-1850?

6. Describe the native cultures of two Indian tribes that show both their uniqueness among Indian cultures in the West and their differences from European-American culture.

7. What factors accounted for the massive westward movement of Americans?

8. Who was responsible for the outbreak of the Mexican War? Cite specific examples to support your claim.

9. How did westward expansion antagonize relations between the American North and South, and foreshadow further conflict between the two regions?

10. Address the following statement: "Manifest Destiny was not an act of providence, but was instead a self-fulfilling prophecy of American expansionism."

Chapter 14
The Politics of Sectionalism, 1846-1861

Practice Test

1. The Wilmot Proviso proposed that
    A) slavery be ended by the turn of the century.
    B) free labor should exist in territory gained in the Mexican War.
    C) the gag rule should be restored in Congress.
    D) the property of western slaveholders should be protected.

2. Proponents of *popular sovereignty* believed that
    A) all slaves should be declared free.
    B) Southerners were too unreasonable for a fair debate on slavery.
    C) presidential elections should not be decided by the electoral college.
    D) residents of a territory should decide the issue of slavery.

3. Zachary Taylor's strong base of electoral support was in the
    A) South.
    B) Northeast.
    C) Far West.
    D) western territories.

4. In January of 1848, gold was discovered in
    A) New Mexico.
    B) Florida.
    C) Texas.
    D) California.

5. To what political party did Taylor belong?
    A) Free Soil
    B) Northern Whigs
    C) No affiliation
    D) Conscious Whigs

6. Pro-slavery Southerners became concerned
    A) upon the election of Zachary Taylor.
    B) that support for state's rights was slipping in the Lower South.
    C) when California and New Mexico wished to be admitted as free states.
    D) about the popularity of the Free-Soil Party in the South.

7. The Compromise of 1850 established all of the following statutes EXCEPT
    A) the Fugitive Slave Act.
    B) admission of California as a free state.
    C) admission of New Mexico as a slave state.
    D) popular sovereignty in Utah.

8. Effects of the Compromise of 1850 included
    A) sectional dissatisfaction by both sides.
    B) peaceful resolve of the fugitive slave issue.
    C) the unsure status of slavery in California.
    D) the South's decision to attack Fort Sumter.

9. Reaction against the Fugitive Slave Act was strongest among
    A) members of the Free-Soil Party.
    B) Conscience Whigs.
    C) working-class ethnic groups.
    D) northern blacks.

10. The League of Freedom and the Liberty Association were created
    A) by Southerners who supported state's rights.
    B) to stop fugitive slaves from being captured.
    C) in support of Zachary Taylor for president.
    D) as political fronts for secessionists.

11. When did slaveholders notice an increased amount of resistance in the South?
    A) the early 1850s
    B) the mid 1850s
    C) the late 1850s
    D) none of the above

12. The influential novel, *Uncle Tom's Cabin*, was written by
    A) Hinton Rowan Helper.
    B) Angelina Grimke.
    C) Harriet Beecher Stowe.
    D) Frederick Douglass.

13. All of the following statements about *Uncle Tom's Cabin* are true EXCEPT
    A) By the Civil War, it had sold more copies than any work of American fiction.
    B) Northern blacks embraced the work as beneficial to aiding the plight of blacks.
    C) It emphasized Christian values as being opposed to the institution of slavery.
    D) All of the novel's antagonists were white Southerners who personified evil.

14. As a novel with social power, *Uncle Tom's Cabin* succeeded because it
    A) presented real characters and not just abstract arguments.
    B) included symbolism which was difficult to interpret.
    C) portrayed Southerners as virtuous defenders of freedom.
    D) never directly addressed the moral issues of slavery.

15. Which of the following emotional themes is not discussed in *Uncle Tom's Cabin*?
    A) the broken family
    B) denial of freedom
    C) salvation for all
    D) the Christian martyr

16. Members of Young America supported
    A) Winfield Scott for president in 1852.
    B) universal suffrage for all males.
    C) the repeal of the unpopular Compromise of 1850.
    D) extending American influence throughout the Americas.

17. Franklin Pierce failed to
    A) be elected president by a large margin.
    B) effectively handle the territorial problems in Kansas.
    C) consider foreign policy in developing his plans as president.
    D) support the American cause in the Mexican War.

18. President Pierce tried to mute the conflicts about slavery by emphasizing
    A) Indian removal acts.
    B) the rechartering of the National Bank.
    C) an aggressive foreign policy.
    D) wide scale social reforms.

19. Stephen Douglas supported all of the following ideas EXCEPT
    A) expansion of the nation's rail system.
    B) popular sovereignty.
    C) the Kansas-Nebraska Act.
    D) immediatism.

20. Northerners of all parties were outraged by the Kansas-Nebraska Act because it
    A) admitted Nebraska to the union as a slave state.
    B) was viewed as a plot to extend slavery above the Missouri Compromise line.
    C) did not acknowledge California's existence as a permanent free state.
    D) was passed after Stephen Douglas threatened that southern states would secede.

21. Results of the Kansas-Nebraska Act included
    A) a bloody civil conflict between proslavery and antislavery forces in Kansas.
    B) a brief period of peace in Kansas before the outbreak of the Civil War.
    C) an increase in the popularity of Stephen Douglas in the North.
    D) the Congressional admission of both territories as new slave states in the Union.

22. Who was an antislavery agitator in the middle of the violent confrontation in Kansas?
    A) John Brown
    B) Frederick Douglass
    C) Hinton Rowan Helper
    D) Charles Sumner

23. Who carried 11 free states in the election of 1856?
    A) Buchanan
    B) Pierce
    C) Fremont
    D) Douglas

24. The Dred Scott decision's chief justice Roger Tanes declared Scott
    A) should be set free, due to his living in a free state.
    B) should be indentured to his master's decedents.
    C) was not a citizen.
    D) should be set free by the laws of popular sovereignty.

25. Which group was the only one favored by members of the Know-Nothing Party?
    A) Roman Catholics
    B) African-American slaves
    C) New Irish immigrants
    D) English-Americans

When?

1. What is the correct order of events?
    A) Dred Scott decision, election of 1860, John Brown's raid
    B) Election of 1860, John Brown's raid, Dred Scott decision
    C) Dred Scott decision, John Brown's raid, election of 1860
    D) Election of 1860, Dred Scott decision, Jon Brown's raid

2. Which event happened after the Kansas-Nebraska Act?
    A) Compromise of 1850
    B) passing of the Lecompton Constitution
    C) Wilmot Proviso
    D) election of 1852

3. Which event happened first?
   A) John Brown's raid
   B) The Dred Scott decision
   C) "Bleeding Kansas"
   D) First publication of *Uncle Tom's Cabin*

4. The Confederates attacked Fort Sumter in
   A) 1858.
   B) 1860.
   C) 1861.
   D) 1863.

5. Which event happened last?
   A) Lincoln elected.
   B) Virginia secedes from the Union.
   C) South Carolina secedes from the Union.
   D) Fort Sumter attacked.

Where?

Matching

Match the following with the state with which each is associated.

Loncoln Douglas Debates	Kansas
John Brown's Raid	Virginia
Fort Sumter	Louisiana
Pierre Soule	South Carolina
Lecompton Constitution	Illinois
Constitutional Union Party	Pennsylvania
David Wilmot	Maryland
National Black Convention	Georgia
Robert Toombs	New York

Map Skills

Use Map 14-1 in your text to list both free and slave states in 1850.

How and Why?

1. Demonstrate how the American ideals of freedom, liberty, and self-determination didn't apply to Blacks in the Dred Scott Decision.

2. What characterized the response to the Fugitive Slave Act?

3. What factors caused the creation of the Republican Party?

4. What were the mixtures of views expressed by the Know-Nothing Party?

5. How did the election of 1860 reveal the severe nature of sectionalism?

6. Frederick Douglass discussed "necessary links in the chain" that would lead to the destruction of slavery. As you look at the 1850's, what three events, more than any other, drove the nation toward conflict over the issue of slavery?

7. Discuss the ways in which the North and South had become very different cultures in the areas of politics, economics, and social customs.

8. Imagine that you are either a southern Democrat or Northern Whig in the U.S. Congress of 1854. Express your opinion on the proposed Kansas-Nebraska Act.

9. As a work of art and as a politically influential piece of writing, what accounted for the huge success of the novel, *Uncle Tom's Cabin* ?

10. Was John Brown's Raid a success or failure? Why? How did the raid change Southern public opinion and what fears did it instill among Southerners?

11. Write a series of letters from Abraham Lincoln to Stephen Douglas that reveal the two men's different visions of solving the nation's problems.

Chapter 15
Battle Cries and Freedom Songs: The Civil War, 1861-1865

Multiple Choice

1. Which statement best summarizes the support for the Union cause as expressed by most Northerners?
    A) They only fought to preserve the Union.
    B) They believed that the cause of state's rights was the foundation of their cause.
    C) They began fighting to preserve the Union, but came to see that slavery must be ended.
    D) They fought to obliterate slavery from the very first shots of the war.

2. Which state did NOT pull out of the Union when President Lincoln called for troops?
    A) Kentucky
    B) Virginia
    C) Tennessee
    D) North Carolina

3. Before the first battle of the Civil War, most people on both sides thought
    A) the war would be a long, bitter affair.
    B) that their generals were incompetent.
    C) their side would win easily.
    D) all Democrats would side with the South.

4. Which words best describe the mood of most people as the war began?
    A) pessimistic and cynical
    B) apathetic and resigned
    C) angry and disgusted
    D) enthusiastic and optimistic

5. In the spring of 1862, the Confederacy
    A) had to turn away recruits because so many had volunteered.
    B) was recognized by the government of England.
    C) enacted the first general draft in American history.
    D) exiled thousands of pro-Union Southerners.

6. Which statement about the draft during the Civil War is NOT true?
    A) The North had to draft a higher percentage of their army than the South.
    B) Certain occupations were exempt from the Union's draft.
    C) Working-class Northerners resented that rich draftees could pay for a substitute.
    D) Poor Southerners were angered by the low number of plantation owners drafted.

7. Abraham Lincoln's effective style of leadership included
   A) his experience as an industrial leader.
   B) his ability to equate himself as a man of the people.
   C) his military background in the Illinois militia.
   D) his stern manner of handling any disagreements.

8. What flaw existed in the Confederacy's strategy for victory?
   A) Their offensive strategy was unrealistic because of the huge size of the North.
   B) They could not achieve the overwhelming conquest that their leaders had demanded.
   C) They did not possess enough resources to stay the course of their defensive strategy.
   D) Their defensive strategy contradicted their desire to conquer major cities of the North.

9. At the First Battle of Bull Run, General Thomas Jackson earned the nickname
   A) "Stonewall."
   B) "The Butcher."
   C) "Old Ironsides."
   D) "Black Jack."

10. In the West, General Ulysses S. Grant employed the wise strategy of
    A) guerrilla war tactics.
    B) deceptive stalling tactics.
    C) combined land and sea attacks.
    D) recruiting dissatisfied Southerners.

11. When Joseph Johnston was badly wounded at the Battle of Seven Pines, he was replaced by
    A) Ulysses S. Grant.
    B) Thomas Jackson.
    C) Ambrose Burnside.
    D) Robert E. Lee.

12. Who replaced General Burnside?
    A) Jackson
    B) Lee
    C) Hooker
    D) Grant

13. Who did Lincoln appoint to lead the now-called Army of the Potomac?
    A) Lee
    B) Grant
    C) Farragut
    D) McClellan

14. Who were the staunchest supporters of the Union abroad?
   A) The British
   B) The French
   C) The Russians
   D) The Mexicans

15. What marked the major turning point of the War?
   A) Second Bull Run
   B) Battle of Antietam
   C) Battle of Vicksburg
   D) Battle of Chattanooga

16. President Lincoln suspended the right of *habeas corpus* for the purpose of
   A) providing better financing for the war effort.
   B) making it easier to arrest and hold suspected Confederate agents.
   C) widening the pool of men who could be drafted for military service.
   D) gaining support for passage of the Thirteenth Amendment.

17. Which action was NOT taken during President Lincoln's first term?
   A) passage of the Land Grant College Act
   B) suspension of habeas corpus
   C) passage of the Thirteenth Amendment
   D) passage of the Homestead Act

18. During the Civil war, women in the North
   A) always retained their traditional domestic roles.
   B) experienced few changes in their lifestyles.
   C) entered the workforce in large numbers.
   D) were never allowed near battlefields.

19. Which state was formed when it seceded from the Confederacy?
   A) North Carolina
   B) Missouri
   C) West Virginia
   D) Arkansas

20. Southerners manifested their dissent manifested in all of the following ways EXCEPT
   A) by joining peace societies.
   B) refusing to join the army.
   C) continuing to pay taxes.
   D) turning against each other.

21. Antietam did all of the following EXCEPT
    A) gave Lincoln victory to announce emancipation.
    B) kept Confederate troops from threatening Northern commerce.
    C) prompted Britain and France to abandon recognition of Confederacy.
    D) increased possibility for British participation in the war.

22. Contrabands were
    A) bans on goods from the south to the north.
    B) helpers to slaves to reach freedom.
    C) hold-out southern plantation owners.
    D) none of the above

23. In the Battle of Cold Harbor, Grant saw the loss of _____men.
    A) 2000
    B) 5000
    C) 7000
    D) 10,000

24. Early in the war, Southern women
    A) were afforded many new job opportunities.
    B) helped the war effort within their domestic domain.
    C) angrily protested the Confederacy's declaration of war.
    D) took over the field work done by slaves.

25. General Grant's effective strategy for winning the war was two-tiered. First he coordinated the Union War effort and second he
    A) emphasized the naval blockade and not land battles.
    B) used a careful, steady pace that would eventually tire the Confederacy.
    C) avoided battles on Confederate soil.
    D) none of the above

When?

1. In which year did Robert E. Lee win in Fredericksburg ?
    A) 1860
    B) 1861
    C) 1862
    D) 1864

2. Which event happened last?
    A) Confiscation Act
    B) Seven Days' Battles
    C) Battle of Antietam
    D) Emancipation Proclamation

3. The Emancipation Proclamation was issued in
      A) 1861.
      B) 1862.
      C) 1863.
      D) 1864.

4. Which two Union victories both came in the first days of July, 1863?
      A) Gettysburg, Vicksburg
      B) Antietam, Shiloh
      C) Vicksburg, Antietam
      D) Gettysburg, Shiloh

5. Which event happened first?
      A) Confederacy enacted America's first military draft
      B) Battle of Gettysburg
      C) Emancipation Proclamation
      D) McClellan was replaced as head of the Army of Potomac

6. What is the correct order of events?
      A) Homestead Act , Atlanta captured, New York draft riots
      B) New York draft riots, Homestead Act , Atlanta captured
      C) New York draft riots, Atlanta captured, Homestead Act
      D) Homestead Act, New York draft riots, Atlanta captured

7. Which headline would have appeared in 1864?
      A) "Sherman enters Savanah"
      B) "President Lincoln Calls on Grant to Win War in the East"
      C) "Nation Shocked by Death of President Lincoln"
      D) "Lincoln's Pen Provides Emancipation for Slaves"

8. Which event happened first?
      A) the Battle of the Wilderness
      B) President Lincoln reelected
      C) the Battle of Antietam
      D) President Lincoln fires General McClellan

Where?

Matching

Match the following battles with the state in which they took place.

Gettysburg
First Bull Run
Antietam
Chattanooga
Vicksburg
Fredericksburg
Chancellorsville

Tennessee
Pennsylvania
Virginia
Mississippi
Maryland
Delaware
Alabama

Match the following conflicts with their victor.

Wilderness
Cold Harbor
Atlanta
Franklin
Nashville

North
South

Map Skills

Use Map 15-4 to describe the progress of the fighting at Gettysburg.

How and Why?

1. How did the North and South's strategies for victory differ?

2. What circumstances existed in the border states during the period 1861-1863?

3. What was the mood of the country right after Fort Sumter? How was that mood altered by the First Battle of Bull Run?

4. How did class antagonisms come to the forefront of draft policies in both the North and South?

5. How did Abraham Lincoln's style and political decision-making provide key advantages for the Union cause?

6. In what ways were the battles of Antietam and Gettysburg turning points in the Civil War?

7. How did Ulysses S. Grant show that he, more than any other Union general, understood how to defeat the Confederacy? What key victories did he gain in the period 1861-1863?

8. What evidence reveals that, in 1861 and 1862, Confederate generals were consistently outwitting their Union opponents?

9. What important effects did the Emancipation Proclamation have on both the Union and Confederate causes?

10. Briefly explore how the resources of the North—population, industrial and agricultural capacity, and transportation network—was to their advantage versus the South.

11. Historians have disputed the effectiveness of the Union blockade of ports during the Civil War. What do you think? Did the blockade add to the demise of the South? Why or why not? Refer to the chapter to support your opinion.

12. Define *modernism* and how it benefited and hindered women during the war effort.

13. What were General Grant's strategies for winning the war in the East?

14. What key events characterized Sherman's March to the Sea?

15. What do you feel were the two key battles of 1864 and 1865 that ended the Civil War?

16. What were the vital factors that led to a Union victory in the Civil War?

17. Evaluate the performances of Abraham Lincoln and Jefferson Davis as leaders during the Civil War.

18. Compare and contrast the roles played by women and blacks in the North and South during the Civil War. How did their experiences either hinder or aid the cause of victory?

19. Some historians view the 1864 presidential election as one of the most important elections in American history. Why?

20. Johnston wrote of Lincoln's death: "The greatest possible calamity to the South." Imagine that you are Johnston. Explain to others why you wrote such a statement. Support your beliefs.

Chapter 16
Reconstruction, 1865-1877

Practice Test

1. During his travels across the United States after the Civil War, Mark Twain observed that
    A) Northerners had made the memory of the war the center of their socio-political lives.
    B) Southerners were so bitter about the war's outcome that they wouldn't discuss it.
    C) Americans across the nation acted as if the Civil War had never happened.
    D) people of the South discussed the war far more often than people in the North.

2. Effects of the Civil War in the South included all of the following EXCEPT
    A) a romanticization of Robert E. Lee by many white Southerners.
    B) a recognition by most Southerners that their cause had not been a noble one.
    C) a brief period when Radical Republicans enforced voting and legal rights for ex-slaves.
    D) an insistence by many whites on maintaining economic superiority for whites.

3. The Freedmen's Bureau was established to
    A) help most southern blacks move to the North.
    B) encourage the development of multiracial churches.
    C) aid ex-slaves in adapting to socio-economic changes.
    D) provide aid for disabled veterans of the war.

4. In the early years of Reconstruction, the Freedmen's Bureau was successful at
    A) permanently securing suffrage for black males.
    B) stopping all violence committed against ex-slaves.
    C) reducing black illiteracy to below 70 percent.
    D) convincing southern whites to accept the Wade-Davis Bill.

5. General Sherman's Field Order No. 15 gave hope to blacks because it
    A) set aside plots of southern land for distribution.
    B) guaranteed all ex-slaves the right to a free education.
    C) established voting rights for black males in the South.
    D) indicated that segregation was unconstitutional.

6. Ownership of land by blacks was highest in
    A) areas that had not experienced battles during the Civil War.
    B) poorer areas of the Lower South.
    C) the area known as the "Sherman Land" during 1820-1865.
    D) the Upper South, especially Virginia.

7. The church became the center of black life for all of the following reasons EXCEPT
    A) it gave blacks an opportunity to practice skills of self government.
    B) it operated as an educational institution as well.
    C) it represented visible evidence of the progress blacks had made.
    D) it allowed them the opportunity to socialize with whites.

8. The first building erected in Charleston after the war was
    A) the local bank.
    B) a black church.
    C) local seat of government.
    D) a retail/feed store.

9. _____ was the most influential minister of his day.
    A) James Henry Holmes
    B) Frederick Ayer
    C) Henry Mc Neal Turner
    D) Horatio Seymour

10. The Wade-Davis Bill was rendered ineffective when
    A) President Lincoln used the presidential option of a pocket veto.
    B) southern conservatives refused to enact it.
    C) radical Republicans rejected the plan as too lenient.
    D) abolitionist leaders withdrew their support for the bill.

11. Which statement would most likely have been said by a conservative Republican in 1865?
    A) "The Constitution does not grant secession, thus the South has never left the Union."
    B) "Northern hypocrisy shall never determine the destiny of the South's future."
    C) "The former Confederate states are to be treated as provinces conquered in war."
    D) "It is with no malice in our hearts that we welcome the return of our southern brothers."

12. President Johnson's Reconstruction plan included all of the following proposals EXCEPT
    A) restoration of property rights to southerners who pledged allegiance to the Union.
    B) requiring wealthier southerners to petition the president for a pardon.
    C) the insistence that restored property rights did not include the revival of slavery.
    D) the extension of voting rights to all black males, 21 or older, in the South.

13. The immediate response to President Johnson's Reconstruction plan included
    A) resistance by white Southerners to various provisions.
    B) opposition by the majority of northern Democrats.
    C) the loss of Johnson's reputation as a moderate.
    D) the call for elections in which southern blacks voted.

14. Black code laws included all of the following EXCEPT:
    A) barred Blacks from jury duty
    B) forbade Blacks from possessing firearms
    C) allowed Blacks to pursue any occupation they chose
    D) forced Blacks into labor on farms and road crews

15. Republicans in Congress became infuriated when
    A) President Johnson took a tough stand against wealthy Southerners.
    B) abolitionists lobbied for black male suffrage.
    C) southern states enacted laws that restricted freedom for blacks.
    D) they lost control of the House of Representatives in 1866.

16. Throughout his political career, Thaddeus Stevens was a consistent spokesman for
    A) implementation of state's rights.
    B) the equality and peaceful coexistence of whites and blacks.
    C) southern whites who did not wish to see their traditions altered.
    D) social separation of whites and blacks.

17. In 1866, Moderate Republicans in Congress did NOT support
    A) continuing the Freedmen's Bureau.
    B) harsh punitive measures against ex-Confederate leaders.
    C) protecting the civil rights of former slaves.
    D) promoting voting rights for former slaves.

18. Congress successfully managed to override President Johnson's veto of
    A) the Thirteenth Amendment.
    B) the Civil Rights Act of 1866.
    C) American Equal Rights Act.
    D) the Civil Rights Act of 1875.

19. Congress overrode President Johnson's veto of which Act?
    A) The Civil Rights Act of 1875
    B) The Civil Rights Act of 1866
    C) The Civil Rights Act of 1871
    D) The Southern Homestead Act

20. Which statement about the Fourteenth Amendment is NOT true?
    A) It guaranteed all citizens equality before the law.
    B) It strengthened the Civil Rights Act of 1866.
    C) It was opposed by President Johnson.
    D) It guaranteed all males the right to vote.

21. The radical Republicans' goals for Reconstruction included all of the following EXCEPT
    A) the South's recognition of the consequences of defeat.
    B) the securing of the freedmen's right to vote.
    C) stopping southern states from reentering the Union.
    D) attempting to strengthen the Republican Party in the South.

22. The Tenure of Office Act attempted to
    A) dismantle state governments in the Lower South.
    B) weaken the powers of the president.
    C) guarantee the election of Republicans in the North.
    D) stop the nomination of Ulysses S. Grant for president.

23. The Fifteenth Amendment
    A) gave Congress the power to remove presidential cabinet members.
    B) officially ended slavery in the United States.
    C) established new rules for readmission of southern states.
    D) guaranteed the right of American men to vote.

24. What term was originally used in pre-Civil War New York City?
    A) Carpetbagger
    B) Scalawag
    C) Redeemer
    D) Roundhead

25. Who started the American Equal Right Association?
    A) Wendell Phillips
    B) Martha Schofield
    C) Elizabeth Cady Stanton
    D) Susan B. Anthony

When?

1. Which headline would have appeared in 1876?
    A) "Grant Steamrolls to Easy Second-Term Victory"
    B) "Congress Passes Act in Effort to Stop Klan"
    C) "Constitutional Amendment Gives Suffrage Rights to Ex-Slaves"
    D) "Hayes, Tilden Outcome Stalled in Contested Deadlock"

2. Which event happened last?
    A) Field Order No. 15 was issued
    B) Supreme Court nullified the Enforcement Act
    C) Southern blacks voted, in large numbers, for Ulysses S. Grant
    D) Fourteenth Amendment was passed by Congress

3. What is the correct order of presidential succession?
    A) Grant, Johnson, Hayes
    B) Johnson, Hayes, Grant
    C) Johnson, Grant, Hayes
    D) Grant, Hayes, Johnson

4. In which year did "Liberal Republicans" in Congress have the most power?
    A) 1866
    B) 1869
    C) 1874
    D) 1884

5. Which event happened last?
    A) Freedmen Bureau closes
    B) radical Republicans moved to oust President Johnson from office
    C) Republican civil rights advocate, Charles Sumner, died
    D) The Ku Klux Klan emerged as a force of terror in the South

Where?

Matching

Match the following people with the appropriate state.

Thaddeus Stevens	Massachusetts
Charles Sumner	Indiana
Martha Schofield	New York
William Tweed	Pennsylvania
	Louisiana
	South Carolina

Map Skills

Using Map 16-1 from your text, answer the following questions:

1. List the states that made up the 5 new military districts.

2. Which districts had the highest number of former Confederate states?

3. Which was the first state admitted back into the Union?

4. Which was the last state admitted back into the Union?

How and Why?

1. What accomplishments did the Freedmen's Bureau make during Reconstruction?

2. Compare and contrast the White Southern perspective of end of the Civil War with that of the Black Southern perspective.

3. Describe the characteristics that define the sharecropping system.

4. During Reconstruction, what factors made the Republican Party a powerful force in all national elections?

5. What laws and amendments were passed by Congress in its effort to extend the parameters of democracy during Reconstruction?

6. Historians are divided in opinion regarding their interpretations of Reconstruction's events and outcomes. What do you feel were the events that best express the Reconstruction period? Why do you feel Reconstruction reforms were ended in 1877?

7. What factors accounted for the rise of the Republican Party in the South, and then the reemergence of the Democratic Party as the dominant power in the South?

8. W.E.B. Dubois stated that Reconstruction was a time in which, "The slave went free; stood a brief moment in the sun; then moved back toward slavery." What historical evidence supports Dubois's thesis?

9. Briefly describe the entrance of Blacks into the political arena in the South. What types of legislation did they seek to pass and why? Then briefly mention what led to their demise as officeholders.

10. Many historians feel that both the promise and disappointment of Reconstruction provided the foundation for the next 100 years of race relations in the South. In what ways is this idea true?

LECTURE COMPANION

The following lecture note pages can be used to record your instructor's lectures and assignments for each chapter.

Chapter 1
Worlds Apart

Lecture Notes   **Date:**_____

Chapter 2
Transplantation, 1600-1685

Lecture Notes   **Date:**_____

Chapter 3
The Creation of New Worlds

Lecture Notes   **Date:**_____

Chapter 4
Convergence and Conflict, 1660s-1763

Lecture Notes   **Date:**_____

Chapter 5
Imperial Breakdown, 1763-1774

Lecture Notes   **Date:**_____

Chapter 6
The War for Independence, 1774-1783

Lecture Notes   **Date:**_____

Chapter 7
The First Republic, 1776-1789

Lecture Notes   **Date:**_____

Chapter 8
A New Republic and the Rise of Parties, 1789-1800

Lecture Notes   **Date:**_____

Chapter 9
The Triumph and Collapse of Jeffersonian Republicanism, 1800-1824

Lecture Notes   **Date:**_____

Chapter 10
The Jacksonian Era, 1824-1845

Lecture Notes   **Date:**_____

Chapter 11
Slavery and the Old South, 1800-1860

Lecture Notes   **Date:**_____

Chapter 12
The Market Revolution and Social Reform, 1815-1850

Lecture Notes   **Date:**_____

Chapter 13
The Way West

Lecture Notes   **Date:**_____

Chapter 14
The Politics of Sectionalism, 1846-1861

Lecture Notes

Date:_____

Chapter 15
Battle Cries and Freedom Songs: The Civil War, 1861-1865

Lecture Notes   **Date:**_____

Chapter 16
Reconstruction, 1865-1877

Lecture Notes   **Date:**_____

Answer Key (Volume I)

Practice Test
1. c
2. a
3. b
4. a
5. a
6. d
7. d
8. d
9. c
10. c
11. b
12. c
13. b
14. a
15. b
16. a
17. c
18. a
19. c
20. a
21. c
22. c
23. d
24. c
25. a

When?
1. c
2. a
3. c.
4. d
5. a

Where?
Columbus—Spain
Dias—Portugal
De Leon—Spain
Drake—England
Raleigh—England
Cartier—France

Cabot—England
Da Gama—Portugal
Pizarrro—Spain
De Soto—Spain

Map skills

Mayans	Central America
Susquehannocks	PA
Powhatans	MD/ VA area
Pequots	CT
Aztecs	Central America

CHAPTER 2: TRANSPLANTATION

Practice Test
1. c
2. b
3. a
4. c
5. b
6. c
7. b
8. c
9. d
10. d
11. b
12. b
13. b
14. d
15. b
16. c
17. b
18. a
19. b
20. d
21. c
22. c
23. b
24. c
25. b

When?
Virginia
Maryland
Rhode Island
Connecticut
New York

Where?
Penn—Pennsylvania
Calvert—Maryland
Champlain—Quebec
Smith—Rhode Island
Bradford—Massachusetts
Winthrop—Massachusetts
Williams—Massachusetts
Hutchinson—Massachusetts
Stuyvesant—New Nethelands
Cooper—Carolina

Map Skills
1. Tadoussac
2. Tadoussac
3. St. Lawrence
4. Quebec and Montreal
5. Huron Indians

CHAPTER 3: THE CRATION OF NEW WORLDS

Practice Test
1. a
2. c
3. b
4. a
5. d
6. b
7. d
8. a
9. c
10. b
11. a
12. b
13. d
14. d
15. c
16. a

17. a
18. c
19. a
20. c
21. c
22. d
23. a
24. a
25. b

When?
1. c
2. c
3. b
4. c
5. c

Where?
Maryland law defines slavery life long inheritable status—(1661)
Tuscarora War in Carolina—(1711-1713)
Second phase of Beaver War—(1680s)
Yamasee War in Carolina—(1715-1716)
Slave conspiracy discovered in NY City—(1741)
First phase of Beaver Wars—(1640)

Map Skills
1. New Mexico
2. Spanish Franciscans
3. French Jesuits
4. Florida
5. St. Lawrence

CHAPTER 4: CONVERGENCE AND CONFLICT

Practice Test
1. b
2. c
3. c
4. b
5. a
6. c
7. d

8. c
9. c
10. c
11. b
12. d
13. b
14. b
15. b
16. d
17. c
18. d
19. a
20. b
21. b
22. b
23. c
24. a
25. b

When?
King William's War
Queen Anne's War
King George's War
Seven Years' War

Where?
War of the Spanish Succession—Queen
Anne's War
War of the Austrian Succession—King
George's War
War of the League of Augsburg—King
William's War
Seven Years' War—French and Indian
War

CHAPTER 5: IMPERIAL BREAKDOWN

Practice Test
1. c
2. a
3. a
4. d
5. d
6. a
7. b

8. c
9. c
10. b
11. a
12. b
13. c
14. a
15. c
16. a
17. c
18. b
19. c
20. d
21. d
22. c
23. b
24. b
25. b

When?
George III
Paxton Boys murder Conestogas
Stamp Act passed
Townshend duties imposed
Boston Tea Party

Where?
Pontiac's Rebellion—Ohio Valley
Paxton Boys—Harrisburg
Parson's Cause—Virginia
Stamp Act Congress—New York City
First Continental Congress—
Philadelphia
Regulators—North Carolina
Dartmouth—Boston

Map Skills
1. Appalacian
2. Mississippi
3. Stop western migration/expansion
4. Choctaws

CHAPTER 6: THE WAR FOR INDEPENDNCE

Practice Test
1. c
2. d
3. b
4. c
5. a
6. a
7. c
8. b
9. a
10. d
11. a
12. d
13. b
14. b
15. c
16. c
17. a
18. c
19. a
20. b
21. d
22. c
23. a
24. d
25. b

When?
Battle of Lexington
Battle of Bunker Hill
Thomas Paine's *Common Sense*
Battle of Trenton
Declaration of Independence is ratified

Where?
Charleston—South Carolina
Moore's Creek—North Carolina
Great Bridge—Virginia
Bunker Hill—Massachusetts
Lexington—Massachusetts
Concord—Massachusetts
Trenton—New Jersey
White Plains—New York

Brandywine Creek—Pennsylvania
Saratoga—New York

Map Skills
1. Southwest
2. Southeast
3. Massachusetts
4. Massachusetts
5. Americans

CHAPTER 7: THE FIRST REUPBLIC

Practice Test
1. d
2. b
3. a
4. c
5. b
6. a
7. d
8. d
9. c
10. b
11. a
12. b
13. b
14. d
15. a
16. b
17. c
18. d
19. c
20. b
21. a
22. c
23. c
24. a
25. c

When?
1. b
2. c
3. a
4. d

Where?

Alexander Hamilton—New York
Roger Sherman—Connecticut
Robert Morris—Pennsylvania
Theophilus Parsons—Massachusetts
George Mason—Virginia
Edmund Randolph—Virginia
John Hancock—Massachusetts
James Madison—Virginia
Patrick Henry—Virginia
Edward Rutledge—South Carolina
James Monroe—Virginia

CHAPTER 8: A NEW REPUBLIC AND THE RISE OF PARTIES

Practice Test

1. a
2. b
3. d
4. a
5. a
6. d
7. c
8. a
9. d
10. d
11. d
12. c
13. d
14. b
15. b
16. a
17. a
18. d
19. c
20. c
21. c
22. c
23. b
24. c
25. c

When?

1. c
2. c
3. d
4. b
5. d

Where?

Supported Hamilton's economic program—FEDERALISTS
Generally supported French Revolution—REPUBLICANS
Strongest support from the South and West—REBPUBLCANS
Supported Jay's Treaty—FEDERALISTS
Opposed the Alien and Sedition Acts—REPUBLICANS

Map Skills

1. Osages, Iowas, Sauks and Foxes, Quapaws
2. Northwest Territory, at base of Lake Erie
3. Delawares, Northwest Territory
4. the Northeast and Midatlantic
5. Chippewas

CHAPTER 9: THE TRIUPH AND COLLAPSE OF JEFFERSONIAN REPUBLICANISM

Practice Test

1. b
2. b
3. d
4. a
5. d
6. b
7. a
8. b
9. d
10. d
11. a
12. c
13. d

14. c
15. d
16. c
17. b
18. c
19. c
20. c
21. a
22. d
23. b
24. c
25. a

When?
1. a
2. c
3. c
4. c
5. b

Where?
John Calhoun—South Carolina
William Crawford—Georgia
John Quincy Adams—Massachusetts
Henry Clay—Kentucky
Andrew Jackson—Tennessee

MapSkills
1. St Louis
2. Fort Clatsop
3. Missouri
4. Lewis was shorter, went north, Clark was longer, went further south
5. Spain

CHAPTER 10: THE JACKSONIAN ERA

Practice Test
1. a
2. c
3. c
4. c
5. b
6. d

7. d
8. d
9. c
10. b
11. c
12. c
13. d
14. b
15. a
16. b
17. b
18. a
19. d
20. a
21. a
22. a
23. a
24. c
25. c

When?
1. a
2. a
3. c
4. d
5. a

Where?
Pennsylvania—Jackson
Tennessee—Jackson
New Hampshire—Adams
Georgia—Jackson
Kentucky—Jackson

Map Skills
1. 1835
2. Cherokees
3. Lousiana
4. Chichkasaws
5. Sauks and Foxes

CHAPTER 11: SLAVERY AND THE OLD SOUTH

Practice Test
1. b

2. d
3. d
4. d
5. d
6. a
7. d
8. a
9. c
10. c
11. a
12. b
13. b
14. b
15. c
16. d
17. a
18. a
19. d
20. a
21. d
22. d
23. d
24. b
25. b

When?
1. a
2. b
3. c
4. c
5. c

Where?
Lower South—1800
Upper South, Middle States—1830
Upper South, Lower State—1860

Map Skills
1. Kentucky, Missouri
2. cotton
3. MO, KY, TN, NC, VA
4. Louisiana
5. Arkansas, Alabama

CHAPTER 12: THE MARKET REVOLUTION AND SOCIAL REFOM

Practice Test
1. b
2. c
3. d
4. a
5. c
6. c
7. b
8. a
9. a
10. d
11. c
12. b
13. d
14. b
15. c
16. d
17. a
18. b
19. d
20. b
21. d
22. c
23. b
24. c
25. b

When?
1. a
2. c
3. a
4. a
5. c
6. a
7. d

Where?
Moral—American Temperance Society
Institutional—Massachusetts Board of Education
Utopian—Shakers
Abolition—American Anti-slavery Society

Women's rights—Seneca Falls

Map Skills
1. Buffalo
2. St.Louis
3.Pennsylvania
4. Alleghany, Ohio, Monongahela
5.Deleware & Hudson

CHAPTER 13: THE WAY WEST

Practice Test
1. a
2. b
3. b
4. a
5. b
6. c
7. a
8. b
9. d
10. c
11. d
12. b
13. b
14. c
15. d
16. b
17. d
18. c
19. b
20. d
21. c
22. c
23. d
24. b
25. d

When?
1. d
2. a
3. b
4. e
5. c

Where?

FREE	SLAVE
Indiana	Missouri
Iowa	Florida
California	Arkansas
Michigan	Texas
	Mississippi
	Alabama

Map Skills
Fort Kearney
Bent's Old Fort
Fort Laramie
Fort Hall
Sutters's Fort

CHAPTER 14: THE POLITICS OF SECTIONALISM

Practice Test
1. b
2. d
3. a
4. d
5. c
6. c
7. c
8. a
9. d
10. b
11. a
12. c
13. c
14. a
15. c
16. d
17. b
18. c
19. d
20. b
21. a
22. a
23. c
24. c
25. d

When?

1. c
2. b
3. d
4. c
5. d

Where?

Lincoln-Douglass Debates—Illinois
John Brown's Raid—New York
Ft.Sumtner—South Carolina
Pierre Soule—Louisiana
Lecompton Constitution—Kansas
Constitutional Union Party—Maryland
David Wilmont—Pennsylvania
National Black Convention—Virginia
Robert Toombs—Georgia

Map Skills

FREE STATES	SLAVE STATES
Pennsylvania	Virginia
New England	North Carolina
New York	South Carolina
Ohio	Georgia
Minnesota	Florida
Wisconsin	Alabama
Iowa	Kentucky
Illinois	Tennessee
Indiana	Mississippi
	Louisiana
	Texas
	Missouri
	Arkansas

CHAPTER 15: BATTLE CRIES AND FREEDOM SONGS: THE CIVIL WAR

Practice Test

1. c
2. a
3. c
4. d
5. c
6. a
7. b
8. c
9. a
10. c
11. d
12. c
13. d
14. c
15. b
16. b
17. c
18. c
19. c
20. c
21. d
22. b
23. c
24. d
25. d

When?

1. c
2. d
3. c
4. a
5. a
6. b
7. a
8. d

Where?

Gettysburg—Pennsylvania
First Bull Run—Virginia
Antietam—Maryland
Chattanooga—Tennessee
Vicksburg—Mississippi
Fredericksburg—Virginia
Chancellorville—Virginia

Wilderness, Cold Harbor, Franklin—SOUTH
Atlanta, Nashville—NORTH

Map Skills

Answers will vary

CHAPTER 16: RECONSTRUCTION

Practice Test

1. d
2. c
3. c
4. c
5. a
6. c
7. a
8. b
9. c
10. a
11. a
12. b
13. a
14. c
15. b
16. b
17. b
18. b
19. b
20. d
21. c
22. b
23. d
24. b
25. d

When?

1. d
2. c
3. c
4. c
5. c

Where?

Thaddeus Stevens—Pennsylvania
Charles Sumner—Massachusetts
Martha Schofield—South Carolina
William Tweed—New York

Map Skills

1. Virginia, North Carolina, Mississippi, Georgia, Louisiana
2. 3
3. Tennessee
4. South Carolina, Louisiana, Florida